DRINKING
GAMES

DRINKING GAMES

A Memoir

Sarah Levy

ST. MARTIN'S PRESS
NEW YORK

First published in the United States by St. Martin's Press, an imprint of St. Martin's Publishing Group

www.stmartins.com

Olives illustration: © Daria Ustiugova/Shutterstock.com

Library of Congress Cataloging-in-Publication Data

Names: Levy, Sarah, 1989– author.
Title: Drinking games : a memoir / Sarah Levy.
Description: First edition. | New York : St. Martin's Press, 2023.
Identifiers: LCCN 2022040407 | ISBN 9781250280589 (hardcover) |
    ISBN 9781250280596 (ebook)
Subjects: LCSH: Levy, Sarah, 1989– | Women alcoholics—New York
    (State)—New York—Biography. | Alcoholism—Social aspects—New York
    (State)—New York. | Alcoholics—New York (State)—New York—
    Biography. | New York (N.Y.)—Biography.
Classification: LCC HV5293.L48 A3 2023 | DDC 362.292092 [B]—dc23/
    eng/20220830
LC record available at https://lccn.loc.gov/2022040407

Our books may be purchased in bulk for promotional, educational, or business use. Please contact your local bookseller or the Macmillan Corporate and Premium Sales Department at 1-800-221-7945, extension 5442, or by email at MacmillanSpecialMarkets@macmillan.com.

First Edition: 2023

10 9 8 7 6 5 4 3 2 1

To my family—for loving every version of me

I have already lost touch with a couple of people
I used to be.

—Joan Didion

CONTENTS

PART III: SOBER

PART IV: FREE

AUTHOR'S NOTE: ABOUT THIS BOOK

If you are the type of person who can party and wake up the next morning feeling normal, I salute you. I spent my twenties trying to keep up with you, be friends with you, and drink like you. I don't judge you for getting drunk and I have no feelings about the morality of drinking. In all honesty, I love watching your Instagram stories.

But there is another kind of drinker: The one who can't seem to stop when they start, who has a personality change when the alcohol hits, who can go from laughter to tears in a single sip, who thinks about their next drink order as soon as the first one arrives. Maybe they think about taking a break or cutting back, but they worry their entire life will fall apart. How will they ever find fun, love, connection, or purpose without alcohol?

I wrote this book for every reader to find something of

themselves in it. Whether you are holding on to toxic friend-ships, stuck in romantic relationships that aren't serving you, overexercising, obsessed with an endless pursuit of wellness, hiding behind your job or your phone, or have a secret bad habit you just can't break—this book is for you. But this book is especially intended for the drinker who wonders about life on the other side. I was one of you. I felt so alone every time I woke up hungover, trapped in a cycle I couldn't seem to break. I was desperate for stories about people who were living—and I mean really living—without alcohol. I wanted to know that, if I stopped, I would be okay. These were the stories I needed to hear, which is why I am telling you mine now.

The following essays depict events that happened to me, reconstructed with the help of journal entries, photos, con-versations with friends and family, and my memories. Some names and identifying details of those I met along the way have been changed. Everything you are about to read is true.

One more thing: this book explores sensitive topics like suicide, blackout drinking, and eating disorders. I am not an expert, trained therapist, or licensed professional; I am just one person telling her story. If you or someone you know is struggling with substance abuse or mental health, don't be afraid to seek out help. It's out there, and it saved my life.

INTRODUCTION

THIS IS NORMAL, RIGHT?

At twenty-eight, I looked like I had it all together. I had an exciting job at a new venture-capital-backed startup, a great apartment in a trendy Brooklyn neighborhood, a big group of friends, and an invitation to a different party every weekend. On paper, my life was on track. But my insides told a different story.

When I laid in bed at night, I felt empty. I thought that if I just pushed myself a little bit harder, I would snap out of it. There was no logical reason for the loneliness that had taken up residence in my body. I had a privileged upbringing, with access to education, food, shelter, and a loving family. Growing up, I had done everything by the book: I studied hard in high school, graduated from Brown University, and found the "right" friends. My social circle consisted of high-achieving lawyers, consultants, doctors, and creatives excelling in their respective fields with the kind of trained indifference we had learned as teenagers. Yes, we were at the top of our classes and industries. But we wouldn't be caught dead showing how much we cared, how exhausted we were, how hard we tried. We were taught to make it look easy; to succeed without bragging. To offset our ambition (and the fear of failure that rippled through every decision we made), we partied.

Put simply, my generation is the "work hard, play hard" cohort. Millennials are the most educated generation. (According to the PEW Research Center, 63 percent of Millennials value a college education and plan to get one if they haven't yet.) We are also the first generation to have grown up with social media. But while our ambition is well-documented, my peers and I were also taught to be seductively coy. This kind of cool was dubbed "effortless perfection" by undergraduates at Duke University in 2003. Students described a social environment on campus characterized by effortless perfection or "the expectation that one would be smart, accomplished, fit, beautiful, and popular, and that all this would happen without visible effort."

My senior year of high school, several of my classmates swore that they hadn't applied Early Decision to any colleges. I found out they were lying when they got into prestigious universities that December and posted about their acceptances on Facebook. In college, I encountered the same types of nonchalant overachievers: a classmate swore that she had botched her MCATs, only to get a near-perfect score, and later, acceptance to a top medical school.

I wanted to achieve the same degree of effortless perfection when it came to my schoolwork. I knew caring was uncool, but there were a couple of problems. For starters, I have always cared too much about what other people think. I also try too hard. I don't know how to pretend that hard things are easy. Every time I switched majors in college (Creative Writing to English to Education to Sociology with a brief detour to Public Policy and back around to Creative Writing again), I felt like I had a civic duty to inform every person I encountered. No one—*no one*—cared, but it was like a compulsive tick. I was curious and passionate about learning, but I lost interest quickly. I needed praise, or at the very least validation that I was on the right track, to keep me hooked. I knew how to study hard, but I wasn't sure how to think for myself.

Partying was the great unifier. Alcohol dulled my incessant desire to be liked; I felt more self-assured after a few drinks. But because I still possessed the same need to keep up and achieve, I was also always "down" for whatever. Another drink? Definitely. Afterparty? I'm not tired. Scaling the side of my college's science building in the middle of the night and drinking on the roof? If you guys are doing it, I'm doing it too. It never occurred to me that being down for anything wasn't a particularly interesting or unique personality trait.

If you had asked me if my drinking was problematic, I would have shrugged it off. I loved partying; I saw it as a declaration of independence and a feminist act. I kept up with the boys through college and beyond, from the classroom to the frat house to the bar. When I moved to New York after graduation, I matched every drink my male friends and coworkers took, relishing the way their eyes widened as I went shot for shot with them in dingy downtown dive bars. I documented it all on social media, watching the likes pour in on my party pics and taking them as a signal that this was normal, right?

My drinking got worse as I got older, and so did my denial. I woke up bruised and bloodied after falling in heels on a concrete sidewalk, but I shrugged it off. It could have happened to anyone! I couldn't have a "real" problem with alcohol, I reasoned, because I was smart, high-achieving, and young. I was also "healthy."

An avid consumer of wellness culture, I dabbled in veganism, supplements, matcha, and anything promising to make me feel good. On weeknights after work, hoping to shed the last licks of a happy hour hangover, I spent thirty-six dollars a pop on SoulCycle rides and heated hip-hop yoga classes. These "power flows" involved fast-paced yoga sequences set to Drake playlists in a ninety-degree room. They became my sanctuary, and many other New York City women flocked to them for the same reason. We packed the small, hot rooms with our work anxieties and broken hearts, squeezing our mats together and thrusting our bare feet in each other's faces. We all wanted a pseudo-spiritual experience that would cleanse us of our sins and burn eight hundred calories. At the end of a sixty-minute flow, I would lay drenched on a mat flanked by thirty other women with the same dreams as me. I could feel their desires vibrating around the room. We were all so thirsty: for that promotion at work, text back from our date, and a hit of validation that meant we were okay.

I threw various words around—anxious, depressed, overworked—but overall, I just felt numb. I tried everything to snap myself out of it: intense workouts, juice cleanses, therapy, antidepressants, taking a vacation, dating different kinds of men, moving into a new apartment. But nothing helped. I was perpetually hungover and spiritually bankrupt, scraping the bottom of a barrel that had nothing left for me.

More than anything else, I tried to control my drinking. Booze was the baseline of most of my problems, even when I was unwilling to admit it. I worked with a therapist to create a list of my limits: four drinks max per night, a glass of water in between each, and no tequila shots. On the rare night that my limits were successful, I felt grim and resentful, unbearably aware of every additional drink my friends ordered. But on most occasions, once I started drinking, I found it nearly impossible to stop. I loved the effect produced by alcohol; the way it made me feel relaxed, charming, and impossibly clever.

A week after my twenty-eighth birthday party, I decided to have a quiet Friday night in. The remnants of my birthday hangover still lingered, and I was repenting. I had booked an early workout class for the next morning and was planning on ordering dinner and having a *Real Housewives* marathon on my couch. But there was a snag in my plans. My boss, on whom I was harboring a secret, confusing crush, invited me to his apartment for dinner after work. And so, my quiet night at home went out the window.

I had every intention of sipping my wine like a lady, enjoying my meal, and getting in bed at a reasonable hour. And maybe, just maybe, my boss and I would engage in a little innocent flirtation. But after dinner, a few of his friends (all European, even though he was from California) showed up, unannounced, with a bottle of whiskey. A beautiful Spanish girl put on a new playlist, and they all started dancing around the kitchen. Everyone appeared to be dressed for a Burning Man reunion, in wide-brimmed hats and linen shirts. I felt out of place in my white Converse sneakers and romper. I doubted anyone would notice if I just left.

Although I felt awkward surrounded by strangers, I also felt a spark of possibility mixed with drive. This was a new social terrain; I needed to prove myself to my boss and be liked. I poured myself a drink and, emboldened as ever by the whiskey, charged ahead into the unknown. I have a cringeworthy memory of exclaiming, *I've always wanted to go to Burning Man!* to a guy in a cowboy hat. I had not, in fact, always wanted to go to Burning Man, but it seemed like what I was supposed to say. One of my last memories is tumbling into a cab with my boss and his friend, headed toward a nightclub.

When I woke up in his friend's bed the next morning with no recollection of how I had gotten there or why I was naked, I knew I had reached the last stop on the party bus. Too hungover for my workout class, I walked home in my clothes from the night before and took up residence on my couch for the next forty-eight hours. I was mortified and ashamed, but I was also brutally aware of the fact that, in the face of alcohol, all my previous plans had been derailed. I hadn't wanted to get drunk, pass out next to a stranger, or embarrass myself in front of the boss I respected so much (regardless of whether that respect was earned). But once I started drinking, it was very hard for me to stop.

I was almost thirty, with a laundry list of dreams I planned on getting around to at some point. But partying was outshining all of them: the book I wanted to write, the cities I wanted to visit, the relationships I hoped to form. It wasn't supposed to be like this. Mostly, I wanted more out of my life than hungover weekends spent cleaning the puke out of my bras. I had to stop drinking. And that's where this story starts.

* * *

I THOUGHT MY life would be over without alcohol. I imagined a bleak landscape of lonely weekends and awkward first dates. It seemed impossible that I would ever find meaningful friendships or fall in love without alcohol. Every date and sexual encounter I had experienced since the age of eighteen had been infused with liquid courage.

A year and a half after my last drink, I fell in love with a man who ordered a cocktail on our first date and looked on supportively as I asked the waiter for a cappuccino. Unlike other dates, he wasn't bothered by the fact that I didn't drink; he posed a few gentle questions about my sobriety before moving on to other topics. After we finished our drinks, we went to a nearby restaurant for dinner. It was a cold Saturday night in Brooklyn, and over shared plates of burrata and fried rice, he asked me something interesting.

What did you like to do on Friday nights as a kid?

I paused. Most of my nights had been about partying for so long. In the absence of binge drinking, I was trying to discover what activities I genuinely enjoyed. So far, I had taken up eating licorice on my couch and watching old episodes of *Younger*—not exactly groundbreaking stuff, but better than getting obliterated on vodka sodas. This man's question reminded me of a younger version of myself; one with a long list of likes and a creative inner life.

I liked to play Scattergories with my parents and brother, I finally answered, surprising myself with the memory of the party game that involved naming objects within a set of categories, given an initial letter, within a time limit. I remembered cozy nights in pajamas, big bowls of warm popcorn, and the way my dad's competitive streak ignited my own as my mom and younger brother still managed to nonchalantly beat both of us.

The man smiled. *Maybe you should play with them again sometime,* he suggested.

The next day, I took the subway from Brooklyn to Manhattan for family dinner at my parents' apartment. It was our Sunday ritual; we usually ordered takeout and shared stories about our respective weeks as our dog, Cooper, waited patiently at our ankles for scraps of pizza crust.

When our dinner dishes were cleared, I told them about the game night memories sparked by my date's question.

My parents perked up at the mention of a first date (Was he nice? Where did he grow up?), while my brother's face reflected the same surprised expression that I had registered the night before. I knew he was remembering how we always begged to play when we were little. How, on most nights, my dad was too tired from a long work week. How excited we got whenever he said yes, fighting over who got to sit next to him. The way the floorboards creaked as we raced into the den in the house that we no longer lived in. His eyes crinkled into a smile as they met mine.

Did they want to play a round now? I pulled up an app version of the old board game on my phone as I posed the question. The four of us, now adults, sat around the kitchen table scribbling words on notepads as my phone timer ticked.

I texted my date as I walked to the train later that night. You inspired me. We played Scattergories, which is dorky but was so fun.

That makes me happy to hear, he replied. Most importantly, did you win?

My brother beat me by 1 point, I typed back. (He always did.) But it reminded me of being a kid and it was such a cool feeling!

Remembering being a kid, it turned out, would play a huge role in the next chapter of my sobriety. Year one had been all about the mechanics: don't drink, don't do drugs, and try to practice harm reduction. Can't stop eating bags of candy? It's fine; better than drinking. Spent hundreds of dollars on skincare products you saw on Instagram and don't need? Not ideal, but you stayed sober!

As I got further from my last drink, I got closer to my most authentic self: the one I had buried in booze since I was sixteen. She was a little shaky at first, and still afraid to trust her own voice. But she had always been there. And the more I learned to listen to her, the clearer her voice became. I took singing lessons, a pastime I had cherished growing up until I became more passionate about partying in college. I went to concerts, reconnected with old friends, and spent more time with family. I even took up meditation (five minutes a day, if we're being honest). Slowly, I began to feel more whole.

I also started writing. Despite my college degree in Creative Writing, I hadn't done a lot of actual writing in between hangovers. Now, I was writing about my experiences dating, working, and all-around existing in sobriety, and I couldn't get the words out fast enough. When my first essay on how sober dating had reverted me to an awkward teenager was published in *The Cut,* I was astounded by the response. I started receiving emails and social media messages from other young people with similar experiences. They also couldn't get the words out fast enough: they had been thinking about cutting back on drinking too but worried their social lives would be over. Was it still possible to have fun at parties and weddings? What was sober dating like? How did my friends react when I told them I stopped drinking? Did I still have cravings?

I had carried around so much shame about my drinking

for so long and felt like I was the only person my age struggling. As I continued sharing parts of my story in other
publications—navigating wedding season in my first year
sober for the *New York Times,* and why I had decided to
quit drinking in the first place for *Cup of Jo*—and receiving more messages, I realized I was far from alone. Young
people were struggling with blackouts, shame, and anxiety.
It was just that no one else was talking about it. I started
saving these emails in a folder on my phone as a reminder
to keep writing, not only to connect with my younger self,
but also as a smoke signal to others who were struggling
in secret.

As I continued writing, I also began speaking on panels
about sobriety and dating without alcohol in my twenties. At
one event, a young woman nervously approached me. She
had been following my work and wanted to thank me for
being so open about my experiences. As we talked, tears
streamed down her face. She told me she was feeling so
alone, trapped in her own cycle of binge drinking but terrified to admit she had a problem. She wasn't ready to quit
drinking just yet, but we stayed in touch. A little over a year
later, she invited me to celebrate her one-year sober anniversary on Zoom. She beamed with pride as she reflected
on how much she had grown in a year without alcohol.
Afterward, she told me that my writing had shown her that
a happy life without alcohol might be possible for her too.

A year after that, I moved to Los Angeles with the man
who asked me about my Friday nights. One Wednesday
morning we went on a hike (another activity I discovered

I loved in sobriety), and he asked me a different question on a bent knee. After I said yes, I thought back to the girl who had been so sure that giving up alcohol meant leading a loveless, boring life. I wished I could tell her that this new life, the one that was waiting for her all along, was the exact opposite.

PART I

WASTED

What I Mean When I Say
I'm a Blackout Drinker

My drinking feels like a fever dream now. The scenes come to me in hazy half memories, my body in a sweaty basement, yelling to be heard over a thumping beat, my mind elsewhere. The goal was always to vacate my body and float above it, watching myself spin out until we both lost consciousness.

I knew, every time I got drunk, that I would not be able to keep drinking forever. The thought would occur to me abruptly, as I was walking home from work in Brooklyn or rolling out my yoga mat before class. *You don't drink like other people,* a voice in my head whispered for years. But I wasn't ready to say goodbye yet.

Until I got sober, I thought everyone blacked out. To me, it was a rite of passage and an inevitable outcome when I drank heavily. I later learned that many people get drunk without blacking out and losing huge chunks of their memories.

Blacking out does not mean passing out. It is a temporary condition that affects your memory and is characterized by a sense of lost time. In one moment, I would be taking a shot with friends or pouring another glass of wine. The next thing I knew, I was waking up in the morning with an empty brain, a blank memory log from the past ten hours. As I drank more and my blood alcohol level continued to rise, the rate and length of my memory loss increased.

Despite the booze flooding my brain and alcohol levels so high that my ability to form new memories was impaired, I still managed to function. I could carry out entire conversations, dance, kiss, and hail a cab in a blackout. When my friends recounted what I said or did in a blackout, I was horrified. I didn't know that person, couldn't have met her if I tried.

Some people experience partial blackouts, or what my friends and I called *brownouts*. In a partial blackout, parts of a night may feel hazy, but visual or verbal cues can help you remember forgotten events. In a complete blackout, memory loss is permanent. I once spent five hours at a day party in the Hamptons with my friends. I blacked out relatively early, already drunk from the vodka and lemonades I had pounded before leaving the house. At the party, I met a guy standing at the bar. Evidently, we connected instantly: I spent the afternoon holding his hand, talking with him, and introducing him to all my friends as my new boyfriend. My friends finally dragged me out of the bar and into a cab, where I promptly fell into a deep sleep. When I woke up the next morning in my sticky clothes, I had no memory of any of it. For days he called and sent text messages asking when we could see each other again and telling me he had never connected with someone so deeply in such a short time. I blocked his number, too scared to confess that I had no memory of our meeting and to learn what I had shared with this stranger about myself.

Even with cues like pictures or stories from friends, I rarely remembered what happened during my blackouts. Sometimes, when I was feeling particularly uncomfortable in my own skin, I didn't mind the blackouts. They offered entry to an underworld, access to the hours between midnight and 4:00 AM, hall passes for the kind of raucous behaviors I couldn't get away with when I was sitting behind a desk. I offered up my blackouts as an apology for bad behavior (*Sorry for yelling at you and then bursting into tears; I was blackout.*) But even when I told myself that blacking out was okay (I'm young, I'm stressed, I'm fun), I felt uneasy. On the subway, I would look around my car and wonder if I had drunkenly met any of the other passengers, or if they possessed memories of me that I would never recall.

By the end of my drinking, I never knew which one would push me over the edge. Some nights I had three or four drinks and woke up the next morning in my own bed, memory intact. But on other nights, when I ate too little or my cocktails were too strong or I tore past the yellow light in my head warning me to slow down and chugged too quickly, I lost myself. A switch would flip off in my brain, leaving my body to fend for itself alone in the dark.

* * *

IT ALL STARTED at a party.

I grew up in a sleepy suburban town in New Jersey. Despite our proximity to Manhattan (*Thirty minutes without traffic,* locals bragged), everything in town closed by 10:00 PM. The main event on weekends was usually gathering in the Starbucks parking lot or driving around the same quiet streets. Sometimes there were house parties.

It was a Saturday night in April, and my parents thought I was at my friend Annie's house to study. I was a junior in high school and my dad and I had argued over my SAT scores earlier that day. They weren't high enough for any of the top colleges on my list. It was the math section that I struggled with, the numbers and equations swimming around on the page. No matter how many practice tests I took, I found myself sweating and panicked, my eraser smudging away my parents' hopes for my bright future. It didn't matter that I was enrolled in AP courses and spent hours studying every night after school. No one cared about my passion for books, my love of languages, how much I loved to sing. My town was a pressure cooker, and our test scores were the only metric that mattered. Relief hinged on acceptance: social, extracurricular, and above all else, to a prestigious university.

A few years earlier, after a string of teenage suicides, my town had eliminated class rankings. But it didn't matter. We all knew where we stood in relation to each other. Your best friend was your competition, vying for the same way out.

That night, Annie and I were studying on her bedroom floor when she checked her phone lazily and announced that there was a party. Did I want to go? I had gotten tipsy once before with my crush, Niko, but I had never been to a real house party before. I was good, a rule follower, because I was scared to be anything else. But now, with my low math scores and my mounting fears about the future, I couldn't remember why being good mattered. I looked down at my flared jeans and flip flops and shrugged. *Sure.* It wasn't how I envisioned my first real party, but I couldn't stand the sight of my books anymore. When Annie's mom dropped us off ten minutes later, the street was quiet. As we walked up the driveway, the dewy night air left traces of spring in our hair. I looked up at the stars.

Inside, the party was tame. Senior boys huddled around the kitchen while junior girls tittered on couches in the living room. No one was doing keg stands or chugging beers. Niko was standing with a friend at the kitchen counter, Solo cup in hand. He cocked his head to the side when he saw me, his face a mix of surprise and disappointment.

When we met two years earlier, I had braces and a constellation of acne across my face. Niko was a year older and always smelled like Orbit Wintermint gum and cologne. I fell for him quickly, in the way fourteen-year-olds do. To me, he was brilliant, misunderstood, and perfect. I thought about ways I could make myself more appealing to him. I bought new clothes, listened to the bands he liked, and grew my hair out long. He said he loved my innocence and nicknamed me "Lil." We developed a friendship over AOL Instant Messenger, and I sat at my computer dutifully every night, waiting for him to sign on like it was my job. He confided in me behind a screen, divulging secrets that made me feel special, but at school he was distant. Once, he came over for dinner and we ate hamburgers with my parents. Afterward, alone in my basement, he didn't touch me. The girls he made out with at parties, he explained, meant nothing to him. I was different; he really respected me. But I didn't want to be respected. I wanted to be wanted.

I relished the surprised expression on Niko's face when I walked into the party. My braces were gone, and Accutane had cleared my skin. As he moved toward me, my pulse quickened. His eyes were bloodshot, and I briefly wondered if he was drunk, stoned, or both. He had turned seventeen a few days earlier.

Levy, he greeted me with the kind of detached non-chalance only a teenage boy can deliver. *You never got me a birthday gift. How about a blowjob?*

I heard faint laughter in the room, but the rest of the kitchen seemed to fade away. I was surprised at how much his words stung. I couldn't tell if he was trying to hurt me, mad because I hadn't considered him before showing up to a party, or attempting to act cool in front of his friends. Either way, he had never spoken to me in that manner before. For a moment I was paralyzed, stunned into a heavy silence. Then, the smirk on his face ripped through my body, reminding me I still had arms and a torso. I reached for a bottle of vodka on the counter and poured it into a Solo cup like water. I had never measured a drink before, hadn't taken a shot or sipped on a cocktail, and I filled the cup to the top. I knew that this liquid had powers, so I drank it like a potion that would make me disappear. I chugged the whole cup without tasting anything, swallowing before I had a chance to gag. When I finished, a worried girl from my math class came into view and handed me a cup of grape juice she called a chaser. I was briefly aware of Niko leaving the room as my vision blurred.

That's where my memory ends, like a tape running out. I have tried so many times to access my mental records from that night, but they simply don't exist. My brain never formed any memories for me to uncover.

Here is what I've been told happened next: once I finished my first drink, I wanted more. I started playing drinking games in the other room, but once people got close, they could tell something seemed off. *You were being too loud and swaying,* someone told me years later. Once the vodka hit my system, I started throwing up. I was sick in the bathroom for close to two hours before the teenagers in the other room started getting nervous. Someone called a friend to come pick me up. No one could find my shoes, so my friend winced apologetically when my mom opened the front door and found me propped up, barely conscious, and barefoot.

You would think my first blackout would have scared

me, and it did. I apologized profusely to my parents. I swore off alcohol for a year, recommitted to my schoolwork, and, for some reason, attempted to teach myself guitar. I was confused by the impact alcohol had had on me: I knew underage drinking was "bad" and that drunk driving was illegal, but I had never learned about blackouts in school. I spent hours trying to recall parts of that night, squeezing my eyes shut and willing myself to remember. But all I saw were floaters, white dots that pulsated along with my heartbeat. My empty memory felt shameful, but it was also a little bit thrilling. I told myself I was *done with alcohol* but deep down I wondered what would happen the next time I drank, and the time after that. I didn't know then that my first blackout had set my drinking career in motion, creating a template in my brain. Years later, a doctor would tell me that blacking out at a young age can impact your brain's future responses to alcohol. *Blackouts become the default setting.*

In college, I used to beg my friends to recount every detail of what I said and did in blackouts, equally mortified and captivated. *You just walked right up to him and got his number!* a friend would share, her expression mixed with admiration and surprise. I was proud of the courage I tapped into when I got drunk, and the morning-after stories were like watching a movie about a secret self, a split personality, an evil twin. I had always been fascinated by pictures and videos of myself: they informed my understanding of how others viewed me and where I fit into the world. I came to think of my drunk stories as smaller pieces of the same collective image.

But in New York, as my blackouts became more grue-
some, I stopped wanting to hear all the gory details. I started
waking up and dreading what I would find on my phone:
the annoyed text messages, the missed calls, the photo-
graphic proof that I had gotten too sloppy. Some mornings,
the carnage from the night before was particularly bleak. I
would wake up bleeding or with vomit in my hair. I lost
wallets, cell phones, coats, and keys. On other days, I rolled
over and found I wasn't alone.

When I was twenty-four, I woke up next to a handsome
man who joked easily with me about the night before. I had
no memory of how we had gotten home or what we had
talked about, but he seemed normal and kind. I even felt a
twinge of excitement as we got dressed together to go out
for breakfast, stealing glances at him as we walked into the
elevator. He was cute! Maybe this could become something,
I dared to hope. We were young. Didn't drunk people meet
their significant others at bars all the time? I started to tell
myself the story we would recite to our friends one day:
*Well, Sarah didn't entirely remember the night we met, but we
made up for lost time quickly . . .*

As we got out onto the street, the mystery man checked
his watch and sighed. *Man,* he said, *it sucks that my flight is
so soon. I should probably head back to Queens and pick up my
stuff.* I had no idea that he lived in San Francisco and was
only visiting New York for the weekend, but it was clear
from the look on his face that this was not information I
was hearing for the first time.

There were the less benign, less charming incidents

with men: the nights I came to mid-blackout and realized
I had no idea who I was with or what was happening. The
mornings I woke up in unfamiliar apartments and had to
ask the stranger next to me what we had done the night
before. The demoralizing shame I felt in admitting that, yes,
my body had been left unattended.

When I was drunk, I would gallivant around New York
City like it was my personal playground. Some of my former
college classmates were making it onto the Forbes 30 Under
30 list, and I was just trying to cut the line at nightclubs
like Acme, The Jane Hotel, Southside, and 200 Orchard. I
bounced from bar to bar like I owned the city, collecting
friends along the way from their Wall Street banks and corporate Midtown offices. Alcohol was our collective superpower. It gave us permission to do what we secretly wanted
to do during the work week: hook up with each other, yell
at each other, and get a free pass for it all the next day.

But I always took it a little too far. I showed up too excited, too uncomfortable, or too overeager. I was always the
one ordering another round of shots or texting a friend of
a friend to find out where the next party was, even when
everyone else was ready to wind down. I was unwilling
to listen to anyone who tried to tell me to slow down or
call it a night. After a college friend's birthday, for example,
my friend Arielle could tell that I was too drunk. My eyes
were blank, I was slurring my words, and I kept repeating
the same phrases. She suggested I get a cab home, but I ran
ahead of her. She had to drag me home, chasing me down
the sidewalk and dragging me out of a bush I tried to hide

in. When we got to my apartment building, I took her to the wrong floor; it took her half an hour to figure out why my key wasn't working.

My shenanigans were getting old, but I was unwilling to consider any alternative. I could tell whenever someone was withholding information about how a night had actually ended (*You got upset,* a friend would offer, tight-lipped). I would apologize immediately, knowing some mysterious inner demon had wormed its way out of my body and unleashed my inner ugly. Toward the end of my drinking, my roommate told me that I was coming home blacked out and running myself a bath. *You said you felt safe in the water and wouldn't get out,* she said. It was surreal hearing my own secrets repeated back to me. *You seemed scared,* my roommate finished, looking sorry for me. I tried to shrug and laugh off my drunken behaviors, but they left a lingering impression. I wondered about the fear I felt so deeply when I was drunk, the security I was searching for in a half-empty bath at three o'clock in the morning.

* * *

When I started writing this book, I had stretches of paralysis that felt like amnesia. I couldn't remember my own story or why I was qualified to tell it. It occurred to me later that this state was like a blackout: I was in my body, yet I couldn't access any identifiable details. Unlike a blackout, I was painfully insecure and aware of the passage of time.

A few months after selling this book, I went to dinner

with a friend of a friend who was also a writer in recovery. I watched her face carefully when she asked about my book. *It's about how I drank and what happened when I quit. Part memoir, part social critique,* I said, hoping the word *critique* would make it sound more intellectual.

Wow, she replied evenly, *I cannot wait to read that.*

I felt embarrassed. She had been sober three times as long as I had; shouldn't she be the one writing the memoir? For some reason I wanted to apologize to her. The feelings of inferiority, shame, and discomfort bubbling up felt like the very same ones I used to drink over. Maybe they were missives from the past; a reminder of why I started blacking out in the first place.

I sought relief from my own vulnerability in alcohol, and blackouts granted me a brief asylum from my life. But the tenderness I felt didn't disappear after I stopped drinking. Instead, it became harder to ignore. In blackouts, I drowned out my feelings in an abyss of chaos. Now, I had the opportunity to get quiet and listen, really listen, to the little voice in me that had been begging to be heard all along.

* * *

I HAVE ALWAYS had the urge to lie. As a child, I told classmates that I had a new puppy at home. I was afraid of dogs and had never even asked my parents for one, but I understood that pets were attractive to other six-year-olds. When Julie, a French girl with a blunt haircut, came over for a playdate, she looked skeptical when I told her my dog was in the other room. *He's sleeping,* I explained. When she accused me of lying, I finally introduced her to Lucky, my plush stuffed dalmatian, holding him the way I had seen my mom cradle my baby brother. *Shh,* I whispered to Julie. She never came over again.

I told white lies, mostly. *I'm majoring in Biology,* I once rattled off to a stranger at a nail salon despite having zero interest in science. Other lies were random, like when I told a crush that I had spent the previous Saturday night at a party with Adrian Grenier (nope) and that I had been in seven serious relationships before (I was twenty-six and had two ex-boyfriends). Some lies were bigger and more serious, like the Sunday evening I woke up in the Emergency Room after blacking out at brunch and falling down a flight of stairs. I had been taken to the hospital in an ambulance, and because I was only twenty-four and still on my parents' health insurance plan, I panicked at the thought of them receiving a bill in the mail. The truth about my blackout seemed too horrible to tell them; I didn't want them to worry. So I told them I had been hit by a cab instead.

In recovery and therapy, I've learned that secrets keep us sick. But at the time, I hardly even paused before the lies came spilling out of me. Lying and keeping secrets from people wasn't something I did to be cruel. It simply felt natural to embellish and alter the truth when my own reality was unsatisfying to me.

But of all the people I lied to, I was the best at lying to myself. I knew my blackouts were dangerous, problematic, and unmanageable, but I was entirely unwilling to give up drinking. So, I told myself what I wanted to hear. When

I woke up with vomit in my hair, I told myself I had just gotten carsick in the cab ride home. If I blacked out and cried, it was because I was stressed about work. When I went home with a guy I couldn't remember meeting, I pretended it was a funny story. I switched from vodka to tequila to white wine to beer to vodka again, telling myself this time would be different. I wanted to believe I had control over the way my brain and body processed alcohol, but the truth was I never had any idea what would happen once I started to drink.

There were nights where I tripped on sidewalks and curbs, the ground rushing up underneath me until I smacked down face forward. The initial contact occasionally jolted me out of a blackout, the impact searing into my palms and knees and sending a message to my brain to get up. I always bounded up quickly, reassuring everyone around me that I was *fine*. I would try to shake the pain off, but once I became aware of it, it was harder to ignore. Uncovering the truth about my blackouts was a similar shock to my system. After years underwater, I was finally coming up for air and examining what was left of my life. I realized I hadn't just been lying to myself about how alcohol affected me; I had been lying to myself about why I drank in the first place. I never let myself admit how hurt I was at sixteen, or twenty-four, or twenty-six. I was ashamed of having feelings, so I buried them.

My therapist once told me that trauma causes separation, while healing means integration. It was painful to admit how many mornings I woke up feeling absolute terror and demoralizing shame over the night before. I separated from my drunk self, disturbed by how little I cared about what happened to me when I blacked out. But in recovery, I learned to make space for the drunk girl in me. I paid attention to the feelings and fears over which she drank, and I began to learn how to comfort us both. In time, she began integrating into the sober woman I was becoming. Together, we started to heal. Most of all, when we woke up, we remembered.

2

A Love Letter to Vodka

In this book you're going to read about how alcohol stopped serving me and the ways my life improved when I let it go. This is true, and quitting drinking is the best thing I have ever done for myself. But before we say goodbye, I want to pay homage to the love of my young life: vodka.

Don't get me wrong. Vodka and I weren't exclusive. I drank anything that would get me drunk (except for gin, which I still can't sniff without dry heaving). I loved a chilled glass (or seven) of rosé on summer days in the Hamptons, a hot toddy with whiskey on snowy New York City nights, frosted pints of Blue Moon beer with orange slices on Sunday afternoons spent trying to meet men at sport bars, and 2:00 AM tequila shots on the dance floor. But I burned for vodka.

Vodka stole my heart as a sloppy undergraduate with

an eating disorder. I wanted to get drunk, but I wanted to stay skinny. Vodka, my college roommate told me, was one of the least fattening alcoholic beverages, clocking in at a hundred calories per shot. Never mind the fact that I was taking nine shots a night and rounding out the evening with beers and pizza; I fell for vodka's low caloric appeal.

When I moved to New York at twenty-two, my heart was freshly broken. A few days before graduation, my college boyfriend, Jack, had drunkenly announced that I was ten pounds overweight. *I'm just not as attracted to you as I used to be,* he slurred on my cheek. *But I want to help you lose weight. You have such a pretty face.* We were planning on moving to New York together after graduation and had spent the final weeks of our senior year lazily browsing apartment listings in bed. I loved Jack more than anything; when he walked into a room, I felt all the butterflies and saw all the fireworks. He knew every part of my twenty-two-year-old body, including the eating disorder that had ravaged it in high school. When we met, I was overexercising and struggling to eat formerly forbidden foods. He held my hand through the first bagel and bowl of pasta I let myself eat in years. In falling in love with him, I learned to love food again. Which was why it hurt so much when he used it all against me.

The night he told me I had gotten fat I was drunk on vodka cranberries at our senior formal. My heart sank, but vodka was strong enough for both of us. It reached into my chest and pulled up whatever shreds of dignity I had left, filling my mouth with words I had never imagined saying.

Well, we're clearly breaking up, I decided slowly, my shaky voice sealing our fate. When I told my girlfriends the story the next day, they applauded my resolve. Breaking up with him, they reassured me over medicinal mimosas, was absolutely the right decision. Only I knew the truth: I hadn't been the one to stand up for myself. Vodka had done it for me. Deep down I knew that, despite the cruelty behind Jack's words, I would have stayed with him had I been less drunk. I would have lost myself before losing him, so vodka stepped in and gave me the courage I needed.

Alone in New York, I came to view vodka as an extension of my new personality. No-nonsense, sophisticated, and smart. No one was going to hurt us again. I graduated from vodka cranberries to my ultimate Manhattan cocktail order: a dirty martini, extra olives, with Tito's (Grey Goose if I was feeling fancy). A cold vodka martini symbolized my arrival as an independent woman in New York. I fancied myself a younger Carrie Bradshaw meets Don Draper with a splash of Chelsea Handler: flirty, successful, and fun. I loved the way a date's brows would go up whenever I ordered my drink; this girl, they seemed to be thinking, knows how to drink. No fruity pink drinks or basic glasses of Pinot Grigio here. I staked my claim with a dirty martini as a person who had earned a seat at every table. At an engagement party for a high-profile politician's daughter, I rubbed elbows with Nantucket royalty who nodded approvingly at my drink order. At a birthday party in an Upper West Side penthouse apartment, I sloshed back vodka martinis as I chatted with high-profile lawyers and Wall

Street executives. At an office holiday party, a coworker and I bonded over martinis and formed a professional alliance that remains intact. Vodka helped me feel powerful; together, we got shit done.

Throughout my twenties, I drank my vodka martini on dates, at work functions, and to mark important milestones. Over lunch with my mom on the day she completed treatment for breast cancer, we toasted with two dirty vodka martinis, extra olives. My mom hadn't had a drink in over a year as she went through chemotherapy and radiation, and I had spent the last year drinking more than ever, bursting into tears at bars over her diagnosis. I showed up hungover to her chemotherapy sessions, and we ate graham crackers together in her hospital room, nauseated for different reasons. When she made it to the other side of treatment, we both felt like we had survived something terrible. The clinking of our martini glasses commemorated our joy and relief.

Sure, vodka and I went through some rough patches. What couple doesn't? On a first date in my mid-twenties, I drank one too many martinis on an empty stomach and wound up going home with my date. I woke up embarrassed and thirsty, with no memory of how our night had ended. On my hungover cab ride home, I fed myself excuses. I had skipped dinner, I had been nervous, he had been drinking heavily too. Vodka felt bad about the whole situation and promised it wouldn't happen again.

The following year, vodka and I attended a friend's birthday party at a trendy new bar on the Lower East Side.

I was wearing heels and a new dress, hoping to hook up with an old flame I knew would be there too. I was a little nervous to see him; we often exchanged flirtatious texts at 1:00 AM but hadn't been in the same city in years. Vodka gave me the confidence boost I needed, and I rode its warm wave all the way into oblivion. By the time my texting pal got to the party, I was a slurring mess. Our friend groups merged as the party wrapped, and we left the bar together in pursuit of karaoke. While I was physically part of the group, I was mentally and emotionally absent, lost in a vodka-induced blackout.

The following memory is not my own; it belongs to a friend who witnessed the scene. As we emerged onto the sidewalk, the man I liked stepped forward to hail a cab. I moved to follow him but lost my balance in heels and fell hard onto the concrete. Because I was so drunk, my brain lagged, and I didn't make any attempt to break my fall. Instead, my chin and jaw got the brunt of the impact. When I stood up, I didn't appear to be feeling any pain. In fact, I tried to pretend like nothing had happened. My friend grimaced at this next part: *Your face was bleeding, and your tights were ripped, but you kept asking us where we were going next.* My friends put me in a cab home and when I woke up the next morning, I had no idea why there was blood on my pillow and a golf-ball-sized bump along my jawline.

You might think this is the part where I woke up, took a good look at myself in the mirror, and swore off vodka for good. But I wasn't ready to give up on my protector and wing woman just yet. Denial is funny like that. A week after my fall, I met a friend for happy hour at an organic wine bar in Nolita. She winced sympathetically as I explained why I had a bruise on my chin but said nothing as I ordered a second glass of wine. We both agreed that giving up drinking seemed like an overreaction to one bad night. I didn't want to be dramatic, so I took a short break from hard liquor and stuck to wine and beer instead.

But vodka always pulled me back in. A few weeks later, I blacked out on vodka sodas in the Hamptons, and it was off to the races again. It would take another two years of messy martini nights before I admitted that my life wasn't moving in the direction I had hoped. Even though I felt adorable drinking a vodka martini, the blackouts that followed were anything but cute. I missed plans with friends because I was too drunk, snapped at my parents, and showed up to work hungover. And while I desperately wanted to make it work with vodka, I finally had to accept that our bond wasn't serving me anymore. After one hell of a rollercoaster ride, we had grown apart.

Like any breakup, I still had moments where I missed vodka. I would catch a glimpse of it at a bar with girlfriends and would briefly remember the good old days. I pretended I didn't miss it, but that was a lie. Vodka still looked good. I didn't miss the blackouts or lost wallets or dry heaving. But I missed the way it warmed my belly and my heart, transforming me into someone who had all the answers. Vodka, for all the damage it caused, helped me grow up. It was with me in my loneliest moments, imbuing me with courage and chaperoning me through grief.

But even when I grew nostalgic, I knew vodka belonged in my past. Once we parted ways, I found the space I desperately needed to become a woman who could stand on her own. I admitted that I wasn't giving myself permission to be happy and finally processed my college heartbreak in a way I had been unable to do when I was still drinking. Alone in my apartment, worlds away from my twenty-two-year-old self, I let myself look at old photographs and acknowledge the pain I felt when my ex-boyfriend called me fat. For the first time, I finally felt how deep his words had cut. They had a major impact on my eating and drinking in the years that followed: I started restricting again and began drinking heavily to cope with a shame that seemed unmanageable. I closed myself off to other men, scared of letting anyone get too close again. Once vodka was out of the picture, I had the space to truly feel those feelings. I cycled through anger over my ex's cruelty, embarrassment over ignoring early red flags in our relationship, and sadness that the man I loved had discarded me so easily. As I healed, I uncovered a bit of humor and compassion in it all too. We were twenty-two years old; thank goodness we hadn't moved to New York together as planned. I had no idea who I was, let alone how to break a lease after a messy breakup.

In my sober rearview mirror, I have been able to see vodka clearly for what it was: a distraction that protected me from my pain until I was ready to heal from it. So, thanks for the good times, vodka. But I can take it from here.

3

The One About Friendship

Chloe was my best friend until she wasn't anymore.

She ended our friendship on a park bench in Union Square. It was early fall, one of those afternoons where a crisp breeze breathes new life into New York, airing out summer's muggy corners. She brought a shopping bag full of sweaters and scarves she had borrowed from me over the years.

The other night was scary, and I just think we should take a break. I could tell she had rehearsed this part. *Honestly, our friendship feels like it's always about you.*

The last part stung even more than the overflowing bag of clothes, a telltale sign that she hadn't wanted to leave any trace of me behind in her apartment.

Can you believe she said that? I fumed over drinks with

a friend a few nights later. *Our friendship has always been all about her!*

Chloe and I met during our junior year of college. She was tall and striking, a transfer student from a southern college, born into a political family. There was no shortage of powerful families at my Ivy League school, but Chloe's prestige was different. Her uncle had run a major campaign for president of the United States and her father was a high-powered diplomat in Europe. She was old-school New England, born and bred in Massachusetts before attending boarding school with teenagers whose ancestors had all been on the *Mayflower*.

Despite her upper-crust background, Chloe was down to earth and charming. We became friends quickly: she was new, and I had transferred a year earlier. I remembered how difficult my own adjustment had been, so I invited Chloe to parties, showed her around campus, and filled her in on gossip. But she hardly needed my help; though she was only a few months older, Chloe felt so much more mature than me. She could be both sophisticated and street smart and had equal parts grace and sass. Her light was so bright that everyone turned to look when she walked into a room.

I had a boyfriend and friends, but my bond with Chloe felt different. She had a way of cutting to my core, bypassing the bullshit, and making me feel like the most important person in her life. She was naturally cool, the first person I had ever met who drank lattes with full-fat milk. She lapped up admirers wherever she went and was as comfortable in old jeans as she was in her designer dresses. We became close quickly, talking for hours and filling each other in on all our old stories and secret dreams. She wanted to be an actress; I wanted to write books. Chloe seemed to genuinely believe in me and championed my successes. She reminded me I was funny, kind, and worthy of good things. We fell into an easy rhythm together, as comfortable sharing our bad days as we were spontaneously breaking into goofy renditions of improvised show tunes.

Chloe thought most of the fraternity boys and East Coast girls we partied with were *basic,* a term for someone unoriginal, unexceptional, and mainstream. I wasn't sure where that left me, but Chloe seemed to imply that I was different, the exception to the rest of our peers. At twenty-one, being basic is a death sentence. I had spent my life in pursuit of excellence, from my grades to my body and reputation, and I panicked at the idea of being boring. I paid close attention to what Chloe deemed interesting and tweaked my personality accordingly.

That spring we traveled to Rome and stayed with Chloe's family at their historic Italian residence. She showed me around the grounds, the orange trees and sweeping city views, and we dined on fresh pasta prepared by their chef. *This is where President Bush slept when he visited,* she explained when we got to my bedroom. Her dog flopped in the doorway, looking up at us expectantly as if to say, *Can you guys believe this place?* Despite their opulent private gardens and art collection, her family wasn't pretentious: this life was on loan to them, and they were happy to share it.

When summer came, Chloe and I spent weekends in

the Hamptons and New York City, sloppy and carefree and deliriously happy. We ate Moroccan food in the East Village, went out dancing, and had sourdough toast with chunks of cheese for breakfast. It felt like Chloe lived life on a different plane, and I felt grateful she picked me to pull into her world. She played music I had never heard before (like a remix of Notorious B.I.G.'s "Can I Get Witcha" and Andrea Bocelli's "Con Te Partirò" that I decided was the absolute best song I had ever heard) and taught me how to hunt for vintage clothing. I had been living in fast fashion—Forever 21 party outfits and wobbly stilettos—and Chloe showed me how to build an adult wardrobe with chunky sweaters and leather boots. Men approached us in line for coffee and asked her if she was a model, and I felt proud to be in her presence, attractive by proximity. Whenever I sensed I was falling into sidekick territory, I pulled my weight in my ability to party.

Chloe also taught me to drink differently: whiskey neat to impress men, Portuguese white wine with spring dinners, tequila before a night out. I had been treading water in heels and light beers, and Chloe was a life raft to a new kind of drunk. She introduced me to the art of the casual weeknight drink, the cappuccino after dinner followed by a nightcap, the sneaky way to get trashed on a Tuesday. Chloe was a lightweight, typically declaring she was drunk after one and a half drinks. It was easy to keep up, and I felt proud of my ability to drink my way from an ordinary night to an adventure with her.

In twelve-step programs, it's suggested to select a sponsor

who has what you want. If it sounds like I lost myself in our friendship, it's only because Chloe had what I wanted, and I was drawn to her because of it. She could be intimidating to new people, adopting a nonchalant, cool exterior. But I saw firsthand how much she cared: about her friends, about what people thought of her, about making something of herself. I felt lucky to be in her orbit.

Once we graduated from college, things started to change. My boyfriend and I broke up, and Chloe started dating a famous movie star. I floundered to find my professional footing, while Chloe was cast in a play and began befriending other actors. I felt like I was being replaced, so I overcompensated. I texted too often and drank too much when we were together, relying on Chloe to clean up my messes because we were so close.

Talking about a friend breakup is delicate; in some moments it seems trivial, in others it feels like too much. Everything exploded when I woke up in the hospital the morning after my twenty-fourth birthday party with stitches in my arm and no memory of falling out of a taxi the night before. Chloe sat in a chair next to my bed, bloodstains on her white T-shirt and canvas tote bag. When I croaked a question—*what happened?*—she flinched, her mouth in a thin line. I had been repeating the same line all night, and she couldn't tell the story again.

I had some very good reasons for getting so drunk on my birthday, and yet none of them mattered that morning as we shared a silent cab from the hospital to my apartment. In the kitchen, Chloe made me a cup of tea while I inspected the dried blood and jagged incisions inside my elbow. I apologized profusely for my blackout, but she was quiet and avoided my eyes when I told her I would see her at her performance later that night. A few minutes after she left my apartment, she sent me a text asking if I would mind skipping her play. She wasn't ready to see me again. A week later we finally met in the park and she cut ties for good.

Her new boyfriend and mom agreed, she said, that we should take some time apart. I was so hurt I felt it in my body, the betrayal crushing me on impact. *I thought her mom liked me,* I cried on the phone with my dad as I walked home from the park. I told him my version of the truth: I acknowledged that I had gotten too drunk at my birthday party but said nothing about the many other messy nights that had preceded it.

Out of everything I felt in the months that followed—hurt, embarrassed, ashamed, angry—I was most overwhelmed by the confusion. I considered myself to be an intuitive and intelligent person, but I was caught off guard by Chloe's decision to end our friendship. Friendships, I learned early, are an at-will agreement. They can be terminated at any time, for any reason. But while I had broken up with friends before, I had never been on the receiving end of "the talk." There is tremendous security in knowing who your best friends are; it informs your sense of self and understanding of where you belong. Losing Chloe was destabilizing: my Facebook profile picture, the framed shot from graduation day in my apartment, the names of friends my grandparents knew; all of it included Chloe. In backtracking and removing remnants of her from my life, I erased parts of myself.

My drinking robbed me of so much, but my friendship with Chloe was one of my biggest casualties. I grieved it even when I told myself I didn't care, didn't mind, didn't miss her. I filled the space she left with partying and made new friends, starting a different New York chapter without any trace of her. Whenever commercials for her new Broadway play popped up on my taxi TV screens, I turned them off immediately, preferring the silence to the sounds of her success.

* * *

MY SOPHOMORE YEAR, before I met Chloe, I transferred colleges. It's a footnote now, an afterthought when someone asks me where I went to school. But at nineteen, the decision to leave my first university and matriculate into a different one felt monumental. It was the first time I had stared down one path and then chosen to walk another, altering the course of my young life. All my high school classmates seemed to be having the time of their lives on Facebook, posting about joining sororities and attending parties. My dissatisfaction with college felt like a personal failing. I didn't know anyone who had transferred to a new college, but I did it anyway. My desperation made way for something that, in retrospect, looked a little bit like courage.

But bravery was in short supply when I arrived at my new school. I didn't know anyone on campus, and my lack of a social life felt dire. I knew I should be focused on my coursework, but I was more concerned with finding friends as a lone sophomore. Instead of studying my books, I examined the outfits I saw girls in groups wearing on the quad and updated my wardrobe accordingly, hoping to dress the part.

Finally, I caught a break: I met my very own Elle Woods. Arielle and I were in the same small education seminar, and she was impossible not to notice. With curly brown hair and color-coordinated outfits, Arielle was often the first to raise her hand in class. She offered quick insights on the reading and took notes with a sparkly pen. I was impressed by her acumen and accessories; she made college look effortless. We began saying hi to each other in the library and around campus, and she was always surrounded by friends. After a couple of months, she introduced me to her group.

Much like in the wild, having a pack in college provides a sense of security and belonging. Belonging to a group was crucial for survival and when I met Arielle's crew, I knew I had found mine. They were bright, warm, and seemed to be having a lot of fun on Facebook. When I was invited to one of their birthday parties a few months after we met, all I could think was: *Do not mess this up.*

The party theme was Beer Olympics. Teams would compete in different drinking games, from beer pong and flip cup to quarters, and the winners of each round would advance to the finals. The teams had been assigned in advance, and costumes were mandatory. I didn't know everyone at the party, but Arielle easily introduced me to each of them. I was in awe: this girl knew everyone. Nerves bubbled to the surface, and I felt myself clamming up with fear. Did I look okay? Did I sound okay? Did they like me? *Do not mess this up,* the voice in my head repeated as I brought my plastic cup to my lips.

Beer has a bonding effect, and by the third round we were all long-lost friends. I swapped numbers with girls and posed for pictures, throwing my arms over strangers' shoulders with a toothy grin. As the alcohol swung my body around like a joystick, I relaxed: I could do this. I chugged my drink and bounced my ping pong ball into my cup, winning our round of flip cup. *See?* Arielle said proudly to another girl on our team. *I told you she was fun.* I beamed with pride as my brain connected the dots: I was fun because I was good at drinking.

Many of the women I met at that party went on to become my closest friends. Over the next few years, as we graduated from Beer Olympics to happy hours, our relationships matured as well. But I still thought of alcohol as the glue that held our bonds together. Without it, the weight of my thoughts cracked the foundation of our friendships. *Did they really like me? Did they think I was cool and smart? Did they like the way I dressed?* Perhaps because of the powerful group dynamic I observed when we first met, I never quite felt like we were on equal footing. Wine helped me play the part of a confident friend, and I spent years relying on it for support, long after my friends had welcomed me into their fold.

I wasn't sure how I might quantify my value as a friend without alcohol. I had internalized the idea that I was fun because I drank and subsequently modeled my identity around being the friend who partied. I was the girl you texted when you wanted to go out: birthday, breakup, bad day, or big day, I was down to drink over it. It didn't matter if I had gone out the night before, had a workout booked for the next morning, or didn't feel well. I rallied with cold showers and shots of vodka, thick streaks of eyeliner smudged across my puffy lids. I was the friend who stayed out with you long after everyone else was back home in bed because we weren't ready for the night to end. We sat in fluorescently lit pizza parlors as the first signs of morning—and my hangover—began to set in. No matter how bloated or greasy I felt the following day, having friends who thought I was fun made it all worthwhile.

* * *

WE CYCLE THROUGH different friendships in our twenties. There are the school friends, the "work wives," the roommates, the friends of friends. I considered Chloe my truest friend, the relationship that felt the most meaningful to me while I was in it. In her absence, I tapped into different versions of myself, trying to recreate magic. I was a big sister to younger coworkers, single sidekick to new friends, plain

Jane to wild-child Brooklyn creatives. There were belly laughs, intimate conversations, and dance parties, but never all at once.

Over the years, certain friendships faded. Others were severed suddenly, rooted in shared vices like partying or gossip that couldn't carry our weight. A coworker and I cut ties after finding ourselves in a tangled and messy web of hearsay, both of us having repeated secrets we shouldn't have shared. Another friend moved to a different city and neither of us tried to keep in touch. At points my friendships felt transient, dictated by convenience rather than compatibility. I spun my wheels, hopping between social circles, and seeking acceptance through the number of social engagements on my calendar. I smiled for all the pictures, but I felt detached from the happy hours, the book clubs, the birthday dinners.

But while some friendships started out with an instant spark and went up in smoke just as quickly, others were a slower burn. Being sober was like peeling back a curtain in my brain; for the first time, I saw my friends clearly. And I realized that a few of them had been by my side all along, watching me tumble through each phase, waiting for me to come home.

* * *

WHEN I FIRST got sober, I tried to hold on to all my old tricks, determined to keep my social life intact without making it a big deal that I had stopped drinking. I arrived at a friend's housewarming party with a twelve-pack of Diet Coke and a large bag of Sour Patch Kids, prepared to mainline sugar and power through the night. But I still found myself stifling yawns as the group left to go dancing at midnight. It became harder for me to stay out until the wee hours of morning, and impossible to retain my status as the last girl standing.

I was nervous to tell my friends the truth. I was still close with seven girls from my original college crew, and we had done a lot of drinking together since moving to New York. I waited two weeks, the longest of my life, before breaking the news at Maialino, an Italian restaurant near Gramercy Park. There were four of us at dinner: Arielle, Sami, Michelle, and me.

Should we order a bottle of something? one of the girls asked casually, perusing the wine list.

I'm not drinking anymore, I blurted out. Three pairs of eyes turned to look at me and I offered a rambling explanation: my hangovers, my anxiety, the years I had spent moderating my drinking in secret, living in a private shame spiral about what I had done or said the night before, wondering who had seen me in a compromising position, squinting at men on sidewalks, unsure who I had talked to in blackouts.

I waited for the restaurant to go silent, for a spotlight to hit me before being ushered out by the waitstaff. *Sorry, miss,* they would say as the other diners jeered and tossed breadsticks at my head, *but if you're not drinking, you're not welcome here.*

Instead, my friends shrugged, returning to their menus.

I waited for the inquisition to start, but Sami asked if we could order a charcuterie plate instead.

I sort of remember it being a nonissue, Michelle shared about that night years later. *I think someone asked how long you were doing it for and then we sort of all moved on to the normal conversation of what to order and who was getting engaged soon.*

She paused for a bit before continuing. *I guess that shows how little we knew about your experience. We were just like 'Okay, cool, Sami isn't eating carbs and Sarah isn't drinking,' but it was much bigger than that for you.*

My friends didn't know the full extent of my drinking history because I tried to hide the truth from them. I never told them about waking up in a hospital bed after a bottomless brunch in Chelsea. I didn't mention how unpredictable my drinking had gotten: the way I sometimes felt perfectly normal after four glasses of wine but could also find myself in tears after half a martini. Still, our friends are our history keepers; they remember the unspoken moments, the expressions on our faces when we think no one else is watching.

My biggest memory isn't from when you told us at dinner that night, Sami recalled. *It's from a couple of weeks earlier, over brunch the day after your birthday party.* I had been nursing a particularly brutal hangover that morning. *I remember you being so sad. You said, 'I'm going to not drink for a little bit and see how I feel.'*

Another friend, Kat, said she was happy when I told her I quit drinking, even if she didn't know the full story. *I didn't know that you had been to the hospital with Chloe or that your partying had gotten more intense, so I was probably less worried than I could have been.* Still, she was relieved.

These reactions surprised me. I thought my friends would think I was uncool when I stopped drinking: boring, uptight, forgettable. Instead, we began spending time together in different ways. We went to Pilates classes, farmers' markets, coffee shops, and movies. We still went out for long dinners, gossiped, and laughed. They ordered cocktails; I stuck to seltzer. For so long I had been consumed with being fun and different to stand out and be liked. But my friends had an entirely different perspective, and the longer I stayed sober, the clearer my vision got.

I was surprised to find that we were able to not only have fun without drinks, but also reach new conversational depths. When I wasn't focused on ordering our next round of shots, I was able to remember the minutiae of my friends' lives. I followed up on first dates and presentations at work and checked in when parents were sick. It's not that I didn't care about my friends' lives when I was drinking; I was just so consumed with my own inner monologue and hangovers that I couldn't give them the space they deserved.

But while some relationships deepened, others shifted in the opposite direction. One friend with whom I did a good amount of heavy partying stopped reaching out once she learned I had stopped drinking. Another friend ordered a bottle of wine for us to split at a restaurant before I had time to confess that I was now sober. I sat across the table from him as he poured himself glass after glass, finishing off the bottle. I didn't hear from him for months. Some of these relationships, I came to realize, had already run their course. It just took me putting my drink down to notice.

* * *

SIX YEARS AFTER that day in the park, Chloe and I met for coffee.

I was two years sober and had reached out to apologize for the ways in which my drinking affected our friendship. Chloe listened somberly as I spoke.

Her eyes were damp when I finished. *I'm so glad you're doing better. I was so worried about you for so long.*

I had never imagined that concern was part of the equation for Chloe when she walked away. I always imagined that my friendship expiration date had come up sooner than I planned, that she had taken stock of all my good and bad qualities and decided that the sum—one giant mess—simply wasn't worth her energy. My words hung between us, heavy on the high-top table, a reminder of all the nights we couldn't come back from. *I'm sorry for the time I threw up in your room, I'm sorry for the night in the hospital, I'm sorry.*

Even after all this time, sometimes I wonder what would have happened if she had shared her concerns about my drinking while we were still friends. *Hey,* I envision her asking, her furrowed brow signaling that, okay, we were being serious now. *Have you thought about taking a break from drinking?* Maybe I would have gotten defensive; maybe I would have broken down. Or maybe I would have listened.

In my memories of our time together, Chloe was always drinking alongside me, both of our faces equally flushed in pictures. But now I imagine the scenes differently: did she stifle a grimace when I reached for the bottle again? Did she dread going out with me, never knowing how our nights would end? When, exactly, was she worrying?

When we said goodbye after coffee, we both made promises we knew we would not keep. *Let's get together again soon.* I knew before she had disappeared around the corner that I wouldn't see her again. As I walked home, I remembered the titillating high I used to get from being in Chloe's presence; the rush that comes from losing yourself in someone else's world. But being friends with a bright light doesn't make you any brighter. It just makes you the person trying to stand in someone else's brilliance instead of finding your own.

Being a friend in your twenties is inherently messy. You hardly know who you are, let alone how to show up for someone who is struggling. You do your best, but there are still bumps and broken hearts. And despite your finest attempts, sometimes you hold on too tightly or let go too soon. It took me a while to get there, but I understand why Chloe walked away now, why her worry and fear and frustrations bubbled over into a heaping bag of borrowed clothes.

I still think about the afternoon Chloe ended our friendship: how painful and important and insignificant it was all at once. If I could, I would reach through time and space and sit with both girls on that park bench. *It's okay,*

I would tell them, holding space for all the feelings they couldn't name themselves at the time. *Your friendship was real. And so are your reasons for saying goodbye.*

* * *

WE'RE ALL CONVINCED that everyone is watching, judging, and waiting to see what we do next, but the truth is, we're all in our own worlds. Sure, this line of self-centered thinking has problematic ramifications for collective responsibility and society. But on a small scale, it can be a liberating reminder that people aren't thinking about your biggest insecurities: they're likely focused on their own. It sounds so simple, but I was stunned to discover that my friends didn't care about how much or little I drank. They liked me for the same reasons I liked them: we showed up for each other when it mattered. We laughed together, understood each other, and had a shared language and history.

There were also new characters in my life. I had never imagined forming close bonds with sober people; I started attending recovery meetings to stop blacking out, but had zero desire to modify my social life. But the universe had other plans. There was Julia, a southern belle who called me for three months before I finally answered the phone, and Virginia and Jillian, bright-eyed best friends who told me about all the good meetings. Deanne, who met me for coffee every Saturday morning and listened gently while I ranted about work, Taryn, a tattooed twenty-two-year-old who invited me to the movies on Friday nights and brought candy to meetings, and Britni, who lived a block away from me in Brooklyn and felt oddly familiar, like I had known her my whole life. *Sobriety is chic,* Britni deadpanned one night after I confessed that I was still pretending to drink at parties. *I mean, everyone in LA is sober.* I knew she was joking, but I was also struck by her words. We had around the same length of sobriety, and Britni's confidence was contagious. If this girl could be open about not drinking, maybe I could do the same.

These women—and so many others—taught me to be vulnerable, ask for help, and laugh at myself. They helped me navigate the parts of recovery that scared me, and we forged the kinds of authentic connections I had been searching for in every drink. And while they started out as my secret sober friends, in time they just became my people. A few years later, when I watched Britni and her husband become new parents, I stared at their son in awe. *Your mom changed my life,* I whispered to the babbling infant as he briefly held my gaze.

As I started taking accountability for my drinking, I began communicating with my friends about what was going on with me and what I needed from them. When Arielle and I began to talk less and less, it bothered me, and I told her as much. She shared that she felt replaced by my new friends and admitted that she had stopped trying. My feelings were hurt, and our conversation didn't end in the type of overdramatic declarations (*Let's be best friends forever!!!!*) that I usually made when I was drunk. Instead, it made way for something much more satisfying: mutual recognition that our relationship needed a little extra effort. This wasn't what my early friendships always felt like, flushed with adrenaline and alcohol. It was an adult friendship, imperfect and real. We might not have been everything to each other anymore, but we could still try to meet each other where we were now.

In sobriety I have witnessed friends' weddings, birthdays, breakups, pregnancies, and promotions. Some exchanges felt awkward without alcohol, and there were moments I wished I could have a glass of wine with my friends, just one last time. But as new bonds formed and old ones matured, it mattered less and less what was in my glass. One day, I looked around and realized it had never mattered at all.

4

Bachelor Nation and the
Myth of Moderation

I drank over bad days, big days, first days, and boring days. I would be remiss if I did not admit that I also drank over TV.

The first time I met *The Bachelor*, I was high on Adderall. It was a Friday night and I had taken two pills from a friend a few hours earlier. We were planning on having a big night out, and Adderall helped us stay awake longer. My friend had a prescription that she abused to study, and I silently judged her every time she shook a pill loose from the bottle in her tote bag. (My moral compass always seemed to be conveniently missing when she offered me the pills to party.)

Our night had ended earlier than we planned, which was how I found myself wide awake in bed and clicking through

Hulu on my laptop. I was wired and jittery under the covers, and none of my usual shows held my interest. *This season on The Bachelor* . . . an ad at the top of my screen beckoned. I squinted at the smiling silhouettes. I had never watched an episode of *The Bachelor* franchise before, but these people looked nice. I shrugged and clicked on the video.

Four hours later, I was hooked. Bachelor Nation had converted another soul.

* * *

THE SUMMER AFTER my sophomore year of high school, I attended a summer program for aspiring young filmmakers. For my final documentary project, I walked around New York City with a video camera asking strangers what love meant to them. At fifteen, I hadn't had a real boyfriend yet, let alone been in love. I was fascinated by the concept: how did you find it? What did it feel like? How could you tell, for sure, you were *in it*?

I asked anyone who was willing to talk to me. A divorced mom of three, a basketball player in his twenties, a couple who had been married for fifty years. One man told me that love was a four-letter word for sex. *You tell someone you love them to get them to have sex with you.* The divorced mom explained that once you stop laughing, your love has gone down the drain. A woman in Central Park looked away as she told me that love meant compromise, something she wasn't always great at. And a grandmother visiting from out of town shared that love is something you work at because you don't want to fail. I was struck by the broad range of emotions that total strangers had displayed so willingly when I asked them about such a small word.

I thought about my interview subjects and their answers as I got older and ventured toward a love of my own. *Love means never having to say you're sorry,* a girl wearing chandelier earrings purred into the camera, coyly quoting *Love Story.* I remembered her words every time my college boyfriend and I had yet another screaming match.

Consistent effort on the part of both partners is a sign you have love, another woman emphasized. When a guy I was hooking up with refused to make plans and often left my texts unanswered, I had a feeling we were not headed toward love anytime soon.

The Bachelor franchise offered a different answer to my question. Dating was a game, it seemed to say, and love was the ultimate prize. In my first few weeks as a *Bachelor* viewer, I was hooked, but still skeptical. I rolled my eyes as contestants were selected for group dates and one-on-ones like helicopter rides and slam poetry readings. I wondered how early all the girls woke up in the morning to do their hair and makeup and what snacks they kept in their communal fridge. The actual love component of the show seemed as scripted as the rest.

But as the season continued, I received an invitation. I had told a college friend about my recent indoctrination into Bachelor Nation, and she reached out to ask if I wanted to watch the show with her and some friends the following Monday. I wasn't really one for watching television in a group—I liked to analyze the dialogue closely—but I was curious about what went on at an infamous *Bachelor* watch party.

When I walked into the SoHo apartment, my eyes widened. A giant television glowed in the middle of the room. Trays of takeout sushi lined the living room table, bookended by big bottles of red wine. As other girls arrived, they greeted each other warmly. This was their weekly ritual.

The host shushed us promptly at 8:00 PM. *It's starting!*

A respectful silence fell over the room. I looked around, hoping to catch someone's eye and smirk at how serious we all looked, but no one broke her gaze from the screen. I helped myself to a piece of spicy tuna and did my best to chew quietly.

Joining Bachelor Nation felt like being welcomed into a secret society. There was a group text chain and even a Fantasy League–inspired tracker in which we all submitted our picks for the final three contestants and ranked them each week based on who cried, who gave the best entrance, and who got the rose. I had never been on a sports team and hadn't pledged a sorority in college, but this felt awfully close. It was nice to be a part of something. And when the blogs ran zeitgeisty stories about *The Bachelor* the next day, I liked that I was in the know.

We were all intoxicated by the concept of forever, and were as invested in watching people find love as we were in drinking wine. Each time I left a viewing party, I felt tipsy and warm. I dreaded the rest of my work week: I was personally and professionally lost, and New York threatened to swallow me up whole. But getting drunk on wine and possibility on a Monday night helped.

* * *

THE SECOND TIME I woke up in a hospital bed, I thought about cutting back on my drinking. It wasn't the first time I had experienced real consequences after a night of partying, but the fear was becoming harder to shake.

When my eyes cracked open, it was dark outside. I was confused. What day was it? The last thing I remembered was being at Spin, a sprawling bar in the Flatiron District best known for its many ping pong tables. Before Spin, we had gone to a bottomless brunch. I ordered an egg white omelet and drank Bloody Marys until the restaurant erupted into song and the waitstaff began dancing in drag costumes. I twirled my friend and smiled for all the pictures; it was 11:00 in the morning.

In the Uber ride to Spin, I sat next to a girl I had never met before. Our group had merged with friends of friends outside the restaurant, and I watched the city roll past me as she talked about her ex-boyfriend. She was telling me about the startup she had just launched, but I was only vaguely aware of her voice as I watched joggers run past us, clean and awake on a Sunday morning. I felt like I was floating in tomato juice and vodka. At Spin, someone passed around a key and a tiny bag of white powder. I tried to find my friend, but I got lost on my way back from the bathroom. When I checked my phone, it was 1:00 PM.

The next thing I knew, I was waking up to beeping

hospital monitors. I reached for my phone and found it, cracked, on a tray next to me. I had dozens of missed calls. As I scanned my phone, the pounding in my skull intensified.

A few days earlier, I had made plans to get coffee with a friend, Ben, after my brunch. His mom had passed away a month earlier, and I had reached out expressing my condolences and letting him know I was available if he wanted to talk. I hadn't intended to get drunk at brunch, so we planned to meet for a 4:30 PM coffee. When I looked at my phone in the hospital, it blinked 9:03 PM back at me.

I read Ben's text messages quickly, the air rushing out of my lungs.

At 4:00: Hey, I'm here a bit early. No rush, I have my book with me.

I cringed.

Just making sure I have the right address. Are you on your way?

Then, forty-five minutes later.

I'm going to head out. Hope everything is okay.

I felt like crying. I looked around, but there was no one else in the hospital room. No nurse offering a sympathetic murmur, no friend reassuring me that everything was going to be alright. Without thinking, I called Ben. He answered on the second ring. I didn't know what to say, so I just cried. He asked where I was, and I told him the name of the hospital. He said he would be there soon.

I pushed the thin blankets off my legs, standing up so I could use the bathroom. I got a glimpse of my reflection:

hospital gown, socks, and messy hair. When I came out of the bathroom, a nurse was standing in the room, holding a chart.

You're up, she said, her voice flat. *Your clothes are over there.* She nodded at a plastic bag on a chair in the corner, handed me my discharge papers, and left without saying another word. I hated myself for being another drunk white girl in the Emergency Room and taking up a bed that someone sick may have needed.

The beige sweater I had been wearing earlier that day was stained red; I briefly wondered if it was blood, then realized I had thrown up my Bloody Marys. I crammed the discharge paper into my purse and put my coat on over my T-shirt. I left the soaked sweater in the plastic bag. I walked out into the hallway and heard doctors being paged. I looked around; was I supposed to go to a desk and tell someone I was leaving? I followed a large Exit sign until I found myself outside the Emergency Room doors. There, waiting for me on a chair, was Ben.

We walked outside into the February night and cold air whipped me across the face. Sirens shrieked, but I could hardly hear them. *What happened?* His eyes were wild with concern.

I didn't know how to tell him the truth; that I had missed our plans one month after he lost his mom because I had drunk too many Bloody Marys at brunch. The shame was nauseating. As I watched a taxi speed up Second Avenue, I took a deep breath and lied.

I got hit by a car, the words surprised me. Later, I would tell my parents the same lie, genuinely believing I was protecting them from seeing my drinking for what it had become. Ben's face folded and he grabbed me, hugging me tight.

Come on, he said, wrapping one arm around me and lifting the other up to hail a cab.

Back at my apartment, he put on water for a pot of tea while I went into the bathroom to change out of my clothes. I couldn't meet my own eyes in the mirror.

Ben and I had kissed a couple of times over the course of our relationship, but nothing more had ever happened between us. I always knew he liked me: he sent me short stories he had written and called me just to talk. When we went out for beers, his gaze always lingered on my face a little too long.

But we had drifted over the past year, ever since the night he confessed he had feelings for me outside my apartment building. I wasn't ready to date someone new, I tried to explain, still found myself missing my ex-boyfriend. He asked if he could come upstairs to talk, but I shook my head. I needed almond milk, I lied, and Ben followed me into the bodega on the corner, begging me to reconsider. I didn't know what else to say, so I walked through the aisles wordlessly until he finally left. The fluorescent lights in the store cast a sickening glare on the scene. I waited a few minutes before putting the milk carton back in the refrigerator and walking home empty handed.

We hadn't spoken again until I saw the news about his mom on Facebook and reached out. I wanted to be there as a friend, I said. I was also lonely. I wondered if I had made a mistake that night on the street a year earlier.

I came out of the bathroom in my apartment and found Ben sitting on my couch, two steaming mugs of tea on the table in front of him. I sat down next to him, and he wrapped his arms around me. I tried to relax into his embrace, but I couldn't get comfortable. Everything felt wrong: his body next to mine, the charged silence in the room as he tried to tilt my head up to face his. Suddenly, I was overwhelmed by how badly I wanted to be alone. *Are you okay?* he asked, but I was too tired to answer. I cried until he got up and left.

After locking the front door behind him, I picked my purse up from the floor. I unfolded the discharge papers from the hospital, where I found a typed summary of how I had been admitted (unconscious) as well as the EKG they had performed. At the bottom, scribbled hastily, were the doctor's recommendations: *Don't drink so much.*

* * *

THE NEXT MORNING at work, I stared blankly at my computer. It was Valentine's Day, and snow was coming down steadily outside the window. I could feel the cold through the walls.

I had finally reached the friend I was at brunch with earlier that morning. He informed me that he had also woken up in the hospital on Sunday night with no memory of how either of us had gotten there, but he didn't seem concerned. I still felt sick. I was disturbed by how quickly my brain had switched off on Sunday; one minute I had been dancing to a Britney Spears song at Spin, the next I was waking up in stiff hospital sheets.

At work, I Googled search terms like *how to know if you*

have a drinking problem and *ways to control your drinking.* I scrolled past sobriety websites—I wasn't ready for all that yet—and onto a page about an organization called Moderation Management.

Ready to change your relationship with alcohol? the website asked. I closed my eyes and remembered the doctor's handwriting: *Don't drink so much.* I tilted my laptop down so my coworkers couldn't see the screen. *Moderation Management (MM) can help.*

Moderation Management was founded in 1994 as an alternative to programs like AA. It aimed to provide peer-run groups to anyone who wanted to reduce their alcohol consumption without abstaining completely. Like AA, they offered in-person meetings. I entered my zip code on their Meeting Finder page and found a list of New York City meetings; there was one happening in Midtown that night at six o'clock.

I left work at 5:01 PM. The meeting was in the middle of Times Square in a nondescript building I walked past twice before registering it. When I got off the elevator on the fourth floor, I found myself looking down a long hallway. A bulletin board was fastened on the wall closest to the elevator doors. Jazz was in Room 1. Advanced Tap was in Room 3. Acting: Intermediate was in Room 4. MM was in Room 6. Actors and dancers milled around in tap shoes and leotards; piano music drifted through the walls.

Room 6 had much less energy coursing through it than the others. When I walked into the room, there were eight people sitting around a circle in folding chairs. I tried to check them all out without making direct eye contact. I sat, pretending to be engrossed in my phone, until a redheaded woman called the group to order at 6:00 PM on the dot.

I had no idea what to expect from the meeting. One by one, we went around the circle and shared how our week of drinking had gone. The stories were excruciating.

I managed to only have four beers on Tuesday, a man in his thirties started, pulling on the sleeves of his black hoodie. *But then I got home on Thursday night and went through three bottles of wine.*

Another woman began to cry as she shared that her husband had been sleeping at his brother's apartment for the past week. *He found the vodka I keep in my closet.*

Their faces were tired and taut. I had wanted someone to tell me everything was going to be okay; that it was possible to moderate my drinking successfully. But all the hope in the room seemed to have dried up.

When it was my turn, I cleared my throat a few times before talking.

It's my first time here, I explained. *Sometimes I drink moderately. But other times, like yesterday, I lose control and black out. Yesterday I woke up in the hospital so, um, I came here.*

An older woman chimed in after I spoke. *Try drinking water in between drinks,* she suggested helpfully. The other group members nodded.

An older man shared how he kept a bottle of whiskey hidden in his home office and had only snuck a few glasses this week. A man in his thirties talked about the drunken fight he had wound up being a part of that weekend. This week, he was going to stick to beer only.

Each share was more depressing than the last. We were all enslaved to drinking and equally unwilling to admit it. As I left the building that night, I knew I would never be back. It was a Monday night: *The Bachelor* was on. When I got home, I poured myself a glass of wine and turned on the TV. The only thing that sounded worse than giving up alcohol altogether was moderation.

* * *

I MADE RULES for how to drink.

Three drinks a night, max. A glass of water in between every alcoholic beverage. No shots. No drinking on an empty stomach. I typed them into my phone and read them before going out on the weekends. But as soon as that first drink hit my system, all bets were off. A voice that sounded a lot like my own told me it was fine; my former self was only being dramatic. I could have another, and another, and another. The cycle was vicious, unrelenting, and self-inflicted.

Bachelor Mondays were an easy excuse to drink, a free pass to pick up a glass of red wine again after a weekend of partying. Every Sunday night I told myself that I would take a break from drinking during the week, but *Bachelor* nights didn't count, right?

Moderation was possible, just not for me. This was especially apparent on Bachelor Mondays. Surrounded by wine and other girls my age, I had a front-row seat to how people drank in a casual setting. Most of the women barely touched their wine; some finished a glass or two. Nothing was more frustrating to me than watching half a glass of wine sit, untouched. I imagined myself lurching across the table and grabbing it like the Tasmanian Devil, pouring it down my throat. On screen, the favored contestants seemed to consume negligible amounts of alcohol; champagne flutes brushed against their lips like fairy dust. The laughingstock of the season was always the one who got too rowdy and needed to be asked to take it down a notch. The drunk girl never made it to the proposal.

These Monday night viewing parties became a consistent reminder of my inability to drink moderately. Something in my brain was activated when I started drinking; I wanted more. I turned to my favorite television shows for identification, but their storylines didn't provide any. Olivia Pope held down a high-powered career on *Scandal* despite drinking giant glasses of red wine on what seemed like a nightly basis. *Younger, Sex and the City,* and *Grey's Anatomy* all had similar dichotomies. I wanted to be like the protagonists I loved: free to drink, fall in love, and make mistakes without waking up with vomit in their hair. But when Liza and Josh had whiskey nights on *Younger,* she still managed to make it to work the next morning looking flawless. Carrie drank cosmopolitans without blacking out and puking in her purse. And Meredith literally met McDreamy, her future husband, during a drunken one-night stand. (Olivia Pope did spill a bottle of red wine on her couch once, but it was because she was being kidnapped.) Yes, these are fictional characters, but I looked to television, movies, and books for lessons on how to live in the world. And when I couldn't find any examples of young women who drank too much and overcame it, I felt hopeless. I was genuinely afraid of where my drinking was going to land me, but I didn't know what life on the other side looked like. I was even charmed by the drunken antics of the Real Housewives. So, I kept drinking until the wheels fell off.

* * *

YEARS AFTER I attended that Moderation Management meeting, I learned more about its origin story.

It was founded by Audrey Kishline, a *problem drinker* who did not identify with the disease theory of alcoholism. She said it eroded her self-confidence, so she created Moderation Management as an organization for other drinkers to gather and help maintain moderate alcohol consumption. Six years after she created Moderation Management, Audrey drove drunk in the wrong direction on a highway and collided with another car, killing the driver and passenger. She continued to drink after being released from three and a half years of her prison sentence. On December 19, 2014, the same year I went to my one and only Moderation Management meeting, Audrey took her own life.

I could relate to Audrey's experience. My fears about my alcohol use had eroded my self-confidence too. I was ashamed of my inability to drink normally, and it affected every area of my life. I struggled to focus on work, withdrew from friendships, and formed dysfunctional connections with men. And yet, I was desperate to keep drinking. That is the real madness of my relationship with alcohol: that I remained so committed to fixing something that had never worked in the first place.

Even though I felt like absolute trash most of the time, I wasn't ready to give up drinking yet. It still felt essential, like a natural extension of my personality. I read young adult novels, called my mom every day, and drank to unwind. I clung to these facts like life rafts because I felt incredibly lost most of the time. I wasn't passionate about my job, didn't have a relationship, and didn't have any real hobbies. But I was always up for drinks, knew just when to lean across the table and suggest we order another bottle. I needed any sliver of a personality trait I could find, and I couldn't walk away from the security drinking gave me.

I wondered if Audrey had felt the same way: hopeless but unwilling to give up hope. In launching Moderation Management, she had likely wanted to form a community of people who also struggled with drinking and were equally committed to figuring it out. But anyone who has struggled with an addictive personality knows that moderation is a challenge.

I once read that Jennifer Aniston eats a single chip when she wants to snack on something unhealthy. I don't possess that kind of willpower when it comes to alcohol, food, and other addictive substances. I can't just have one piece of candy. I want more, and I want it every night. If I keep sour straws or gummy bears in the house, I will think about them all day, waiting in the cupboard for me, until I can rip the bag open. I'll savor them, chewing silently, pretending this means I'm a mindful eater and not fiending for sugar.

The first time I tasted a strawberry, I was three. The fruit was so delicious that I snuck handfuls when my parents weren't looking, devouring the berries until I made myself sick. One of my earliest memories is from that night: lying on the couch, queasy, with berry stains on my fingers. I couldn't understand how something that tasted so good had wound up making me feel so bad.

* * *

SOMETHING ELSE HAPPENED as I continued watching *The Bachelor* over the years: I started to believe in it. At first, I scoffed when castmates said they were *there for the right reasons*. My reasons for attending watch parties were to drink wine and make friends, and I found it hard to believe that contestants didn't have similar goals. But as more couples on the show started to form relationships, I began to wonder if this was the way people fell in love: quickly, on television, and with a mutual sense of urgency. When I watched love interests get eliminated, I felt nerves ricochet in my stomach. I always reached for another glass of wine, unwilling to ask myself the question that kept coming up: if these beautiful people can't find love, how will I?

This reality television effect spanned across other categories, from love and relationships to alcohol and partying. I felt the most at home when I watched the Real Housewives franchise on Bravo. These were women who drank the same way I did. I fell into a trance as I watched them get dolled up for yet another party, downing strong, signature cocktails. The alcohol kicked in at the same time as the drama, creating amazing television and even better icons. Unlike many of the contestants on *The Bachelor,* the women on *Real Housewives* were established, successful, and wealthy. I associated drinking like they did with being chic and fun. They represented an era of aspirational rich moms drinking white wine at lunch and attending fabulous parties every night. Of course, there were the outliers. When housewives exited the show to attend rehab or talked about their struggles with drugs and alcohol on the show, I was always intrigued. But I glossed past their storylines, telling myself that my drinking was far more innocent than theirs.

Watching other people drink, date, fall in love, and fall apart from my couch gave me a new vantage point. I felt safe there; it was much easier to sit and judge everyone else than it would have been to take a good, hard look at myself.

* * *

THREE MONTHS AFTER I tried Moderation Management, I attempted to abstain from alcohol entirely. I had blacked out again, and this time I lost my wallet and apartment keys. The night was messy enough to inspire me to take a break from partying, and after two weeks I started to feel some relief.

Today was a good day, I wrote in my journal that April. *Fourteen days with no alcohol! The past two weeks have been scary, but I'm starting to see some of the benefits of living a sober life.*

Overall, though, I continued, my handwriting getting sloppier as I wrote quicker. *I'm pretty sure I don't have a real drinking problem. I know I've been depending on and abusing alcohol. I've been blacking out, throwing up, and numbing myself. I've been hospitalized twice. It's been a dark period. But I don't think I need to stay sober. I feel like a lot of my issues (blacking out, hangovers) could apply to almost everyone I knew in college.*

I guess I just wish there was someone who could tell me if this was a real alcohol problem or not. This has all been so confusing because I don't know if I'm being insane or if I really need help with my drinking.

A day later, I wrote again. *Today I got to enjoy a sober Saturday without a hangover. I really hope to someday be able to have one drink with a boyfriend. I don't want to be creating a problem where there isn't one. I'm not sure when I'll start drinking again, but I'm hoping this break will help me learn my limits. Like, one glass of wine at dinner.*

I think what I want to gain from this period of sobriety is an understanding of how and why I drink heavily and to be more caring with myself. I see now that my actions aren't the ones of someone who cares about being alive. I've put myself in scary situations as a drunk girl in the city and I can truly say that I'm ready to be done.

The rest of the notebook is empty: I drank again a few days later. I went into that first night with a conscious intention to drink, eyes wide open. I set my limits in advance (*one glass of wine at dinner ONLY*), but I still woke up the next morning with a faded stamp on my hand and a paper band dangling from my wrist. Once I started drinking, the inner life I was cultivating vanished. With it went my desire to abstain or even moderate. I pushed the last two weeks out of my memory and hid the journal in an old shoebox.

It took me three years to give sobriety another real chance. In the months before I finally admitted I needed to get sober for good, I started feeling sick and rundown all the time. I woke up in the middle of the night with stomachaches and raging anxiety. I attempted to recommit to *wellness*: I bought a new journal and started logging every bite of food and sip of alcohol. I tried counting lengths of time without a blackout, but usually restarted my day count after a week.

My journal entries leading up to the last night I drank were short, desperate missives. *Green juice before Pilates. Kale salad. Almonds. Tons of water!!!* Whenever I drank, my entries went off the rails. *Seven drinks (vodka soda). Spinach artichoke dip, half a truffle grilled cheese, French fries at Lauren's birthday. Next day I walked twenty-five blocks and went to the gym. Felt sick and out of control.*

It was clear that, when it came to me, moderation was a myth. And after a decade of struggling, I was finally ready to admit it.

* * *

YEARS OF TRIAL and error had proven that I had a hard time maintaining continuous sobriety by myself. So, when I was twenty-eight, I found a recovery meeting for women who were trying to get sober. The room was warm, bright, and full of young people who were living big lives without alcohol. I desperately wanted the freedom they had, which was how I came to decide that this group would be essential if I wanted to stay sober this time around. There was just one problem: the meeting happened on Monday nights at 8:00 PM: the same time as *The Bachelor*.

After six years of dramatic twists, tearful confessionals, and broken hearts, I had to say goodbye to Bachelor Nation. The next step in my lifelong attempt at understanding love would be this commitment to a new form of radical self-love. I needed to step into a new routine with a different kind of community. This one didn't have trays of sushi or bottles of wine, but it offered a chance at a deeper kind of sisterhood and belonging.

My struggles with moderation taught me that I needed to commit completely when it came to not drinking. If recovery was going to help me heal the parts of myself that I thought were unlovable, I had to stop fighting it and start being honest. At times, this meant apologizing to the people I had hurt along the way, individuals who had gotten caught in the crossfires of my twenties. Some of them met me with compassion and understanding. Others, like Ben, had moved on and didn't want to look back. This was painful for my ego to accept, but in time I learned that the best way to right these wrongs was to stay sober.

Sometimes, recovery simply meant showing up, day after day, and watching the ways in which my world changed without alcohol. As I walked to the subway every Monday after my meeting, the night air breathed new life into me. The week was just beginning, and I wasn't dreading it anymore.

PART II

HUNGOVER

5

How I Was Influenced
by an Influencer

My neighbor, the influencer, gave me a pair of jeans that were four sizes too small.

I stood in my kitchen, turning the denim over in my hands, unsure of what to do next. I could try to squeeze them on and wind up in tears. I could donate them and watch the clerk's eyes widen as she registered that these were unworn designer jeans, tags still intact. Or I could list them online, collect the $230 they were worth, and use it to buy clothes that fit properly.

Instead, I held the pants out in front of me, inspecting the circumference of the waistband. At my smallest, when I was restricting my food intake and weighing myself daily, I still could not fit into jeans this size. We were in double zero territory, a domain reserved for models and the genetically blessed. I had briefly visited the land of size fours before setting up camp with the sixes and eights. For years, I determined my self-worth by my measurements. If a smaller size fit me, I was euphoric. On days when I needed to size up, a dark cloud appeared. I was stupid, puffy, a clogged trash chute. I was willing to try anything to live with the smalls, and I did. I starved myself, ran until my knees ached, drank laxative teas, took appetite suppressants, counted macros and calories, and purged.

Small was synonymous with every wonderful adjective I could imagine: smart, loveable, successful. I would pass a thin girl on the street and write her life story from start to finish. She was organized, motivated, and bubbly. She attracted friends and romantic partners naturally and emanated an easy confidence. She was never constipated, starving, or uncomfortable. She was small, so her life was perfect.

I studied the pants and the number stitched into their tag. In therapy, I had been working on embracing my inner child. I glanced over at the picture of my younger self on my bookshelf, chubby thighs, dimpled knees, and beaming face smiling back at me. I could starve her in pursuit of smallness, or I could toss the pants. I folded the jeans up, placed them in a bag, and tucked them away in my closet. Just like the final months of my drinking, I wasn't ready to do what needed to be done yet. I wasn't ready to choose.

* * *

I MET THE influencer a year before I quit drinking. Victoria lived a block away and was small and stylish, the kind of pretty you study up-close. We started out as acquaintances after we met at the coworking space I worked out of in Brooklyn. She was a year younger than me but seemed so much more put together. Her apartment was professionally decorated, and her hair and makeup were always perfect. She asked her boyfriend what he wanted for dinner every night, then actually cooked it. Her boyfriend described her as *the coolest person I know.* I never saw her wear the same outfit twice.

Over time, we became friends. I ran into her around the neighborhood, her espresso on ice in hand, and we started following each other on Instagram. She had 16K followers at the time, largely due to her older sister, a popular lifestyle blogger with over a million followers. Victoria mostly posted pictures of her outfits, a mix of vintage finds and high-end items, and did makeup tutorials. When she and her boyfriend got engaged, he told her she could quit her day job and become a full-time influencer.

At the time, influencer posts were shifting from sidewalk outfit pictures to sponsored content backed by big budgets. Major brands were pumping money into digital talent, turning social media platforms into viable sales channels. I witnessed the evolution from my seat on the branding side: I launched my company's first paid influencer campaigns and watched with surprise as they exceeded our sales expectations. People were buying what influencers were selling.

I started following a handful of influencers (in the name of research, of course) and familiarized myself with key players in fashion, beauty, and fitness. Victoria's boyfriend was right: there was something undeniably cool about her, and the likes and comments on her posts reflected it. Unlike other influencers, Victoria's posts and captions weren't flooded with hashtags or exclamation points. She was minimalistic but funny, aspirational but relatable. Between her cool approach and well-known sister, her follower count seemed to grow daily.

A few months after we met, she started gifting me hand-me-downs and freebies from brands. Whenever she texted, I knew she was opening packages or cleaning out her closet. She passed on her old coats, sweaters, shoes, shampoo, makeup, T-shirts, a tea kettle, and even a couch. My friends raised their eyebrows when I mentioned I had acquired a new pair of sandals or bottle of moisturizer from my neighbor. I could afford my own clothes and beauty products, but Victoria's old items felt curated. It was like shopping in a stylist's closet and snagging the items she didn't want.

I didn't care when the clothes were two seasons old, or the products were gently used. I knew that, at some point, they had been in style and that was enough. When Victoria gave me an old pair of white Velcro sneakers, I paired them with everything: jeans, dresses, yoga pants. I wore them on dates and to dinners with friends. I wore them until the soles whittled down to nothing and the heel tab started to rip apart. Then, I took them to a shoe repair store around the corner from my Brooklyn apartment and had them fixed so I could wear them some more. This excessive behavior mirrored my drinking: once I found something I liked, it was hard to stop.

As Victoria and I started spending more time together, her social media following continued to grow. When she reached 75K followers, she invited me to her apartment to film herself doing my makeup. *My followers have already seen me do my own,* she explained like this was obvious. I sat very still in her kitchen as she painted my face and shouted out the brands she was using (*I'll include a swipe-up link at the end!*). It took me approximately twenty Neutrogena wipes to remove all the foundation from my face that night, but it had been worth it. When a girl from high school I hadn't spoken to in ten years messaged me about the post and asked how I knew Victoria, I felt special.

Social media influencers are not traditional celebrities, but they're not ordinary people either. On one level, I knew that simply having a large social media following did not make someone more important. But being around Victoria had a distorting effect. Her life seemed charmed, and I was fascinated. Packages magically arrived on her doorstep. She wore monochromatic all-white outfits and didn't spill on them. And she seemed to possess the rule book on what was and wasn't cool. When I asked her what I should wear to a friend's wedding, she listed brands I had never even heard of. *Whatever you do, just don't go to Bloomingdale's. We're not in fifth grade, you know?* I laughed like this was obvious, and quickly closed the open Bloomingdale's tabs in my browser.

A few months later, on her birthday, she invited me to drop by her party later that night. It was a casual text, and she likely wouldn't have noticed if I didn't show. But being included felt significant. My friends already had plans, so

I sent out a few last-minute text messages to men I occasionally hooked up with, asking if they wanted to come with me. The ones who responded all said they were busy. This is the part where I should have reassessed the situation: I could have just joined my friends or, heaven forbid, stayed in for the night. But I was twenty-seven and desperate to be cool. I poured myself a large glass of wine, applied another coat of mascara, and went off to the party by myself.

On my way to the nightclub, I told myself lies. *It's cool to go alone! It shows you're confident!* But I felt shaky and anxious. I slid past the roped line and gave Victoria's name to the bouncer, lowering my head as he asked how many people were with me. *Just one.*

Inside, I moved through the throngs of bodies, trying to find Victoria. I knew what she was wearing because she had already posted a picture of her sparkly dress on Instagram. I scanned the crowd for sequins, but it was too dark to make out anything but silhouettes. I stopped at the bar and ordered a vodka soda for courage.

When I finally found Victoria, I was surprised by how small her group was. *A lot of people left after dinner,* she screamed over the music. I said hello to her now-husband, her sister's assistant, and a couple of friends. Later, when I watched her Instagram stories from the night, I noticed how the videos made the party seem bigger.

Everyone was dancing, so I stood off to the side and tried to remember how to move naturally. I had another drink, hoping it would summon my confidence and spontaneity, but it did nothing. I felt awkward and thirsty. *My friends all had plans tonight,* I told Victoria's husband as he walked off to order another beer. After an hour, I slipped out unnoticed. I felt foolish for going in the first place. Outside, I found a text from one of the men I had texted earlier, asking if he could come over. When I said yes, he told me he was already on his way. He had known I was a sure thing.

* * *

THE WHEELS ON my party bus were slowing down. I never admitted it out loud, but I knew I was approaching the end of my drinking career. I went out with my roommate on Friday and Saturday nights, bar hopping until we blacked out and ordered nachos. I spent Sundays on my couch, the stench of alcohol seeping from my pores as I swiped through social media posts.

Victoria shared pictures of her weekend mornings looking rested and fresh faced. *Sunday mood,* she captioned a photo of her at brunch, lazily holding an iced coffee and wearing a dress and handbag that cost more than my rent. She possessed the freedom I was seeking: the ability to wake up and get dressed without a hangover clouding your vision. I desperately wanted to cross over into the land of the free: the smalls, the sobers, anywhere but me.

I lived outside my body, my lungs subsisting on influence. I drank to feel alive, but I also breathed in men for validation, Instagram for clothes, and YouTube for beauty. I was a vessel for ad sales and swipe-up links, disgusted by anything I picked out myself. Unless it had been vetted by someone else, it was trash. Even my socks were wrong. By the time I quit drinking, I barely knew who I was.

In early sobriety, none of that changed. If anything, my detachment from myself was more acute without alcohol. I was saving money on drinks, late night cabs, and greasy hangover food, so I spent it on whatever the Internet told me to. Every time I came home from work and found a new package waiting, I was convinced it would fix me. This curling iron/shirt/exfoliant would change everything. But when I ripped the box open and pushed past the tissue, all I found was an object. *Hi,* I thought about writing to customer service. *I received my eyebrow gel, but it didn't change my life.* The magic I saw on my screen was missing.

Shortly after I quit drinking, Victoria asked for my help planning her husband's thirtieth birthday party.

Isn't this the sort of thing an assistant is supposed to do? my friend Nina complained as I dragged her to look at a potential venue on a Friday night. Victoria would have gone herself, I explained, but she had plans. Plus, we were friends. Nina rolled her eyes.

In the weeks leading up to the party, I maintained my side hustle as Victoria's event planner and personal assistant. I stepped out of work meetings to call restaurants, collected emails for the guest list, and followed up on RSVPs. I even bought a new dress for the big event, a night that had absolutely nothing to do with me. In addition to the party itself, Victoria had another birthday surprise planned. She had flown her husband's younger sister to New York for the soirée.

The night of the party, I got to the bar early to help with

setup. It was one of my first big parties without alcohol, so I busied myself with laying out snacks and welcoming guests. This time, I wouldn't feel as out of place as I had at Victoria's last party: I had a job to do. I greeted friends and family members with the delusional enthusiasm of someone who doesn't realize she's not a part of the in-crowd. When the husband's younger sister arrived, she asked me where she should wait until the reveal. I glanced around the small back room we had rented out. Victoria hadn't given me instructions on this part. Is my mom there with the cake? Victoria texted at the same moment. When I looked up from my phone, the sister was gone.

Twenty minutes later, Victoria and her husband arrived at the party. I filmed the surprise like a mother recording her child's first steps. I was fully invested in the success of his party; I really wanted it to go well. As Victoria and her husband started greeting friends, his younger sister appeared by my side again. *Should I go over there or wait here?*

I told her to wait. Victoria's husband caught my eye, and I moved in his direction. *Happy birthday!* I exclaimed as I gave him a quick hug. Then, I made a mistake. I pointed in his sister's direction.

As he spotted his sister, he took off to envelop her in a bear hug. I turned my back to give them privacy.

All at once, Victoria was at my side. *Who told him she was here?* She looked angry. My face burned with shame. I knew she should have been the one to reveal the surprise; she was the one who had organized it. She hadn't even gotten to film his reaction.

She made her way over to her husband and whispered in his ear. When he responded, she briefly turned to look at me. I could feel the air in the room change. An invisible wall went up between us, and as she turned her back to me, I knew that something had shifted. She ignored me for the rest of the party.

As I walked home that night, tears springing up before I could talk myself out of them, I berated myself for being so stupid. I didn't know why I had done it. Maybe I had wanted to seem important, to be on the receiving end of accolades. Maybe I had wanted to take back a little bit of the agency I had been conceding in this relationship. Or maybe I had just been overwhelmed and acted without thinking. Either way, I was ashamed of my behavior. I had inserted myself where I didn't belong, and I didn't even understand why. Like Victoria's party the previous year, I felt foolish for being there. But this time, I couldn't mask these feelings with alcohol.

The following morning, as I watched Victoria's coverage of the party on social media, I noticed how careful she had been. Like her own birthday, she had filmed selective corners of the room, creating an illusion that the event was both exclusive and well-attended. She filtered the pictures and added captions about what a perfect night it had been. As I scrolled through Instagram, I studied posts from other influencers I followed. Even the seemingly candid ones, I knew, were posing for the camera. What did it mean, I wondered, to be so influenced by people who were faking it?

I thought back to the two birthday parties I had attended for Victoria. I had left each event feeling small and embarrassed. It occurred to me that, despite her influence, maybe Victoria wasn't someone I felt good around. I told myself we were genuinely friends and that Victoria liked me because I was different from other girls in her social circle. But now, as I replayed our past conversations, I realized how little she knew about me. I hardly shared about my own life, and she rarely asked. Most of the time, when I was in Victoria's presence, it was all about her. It wasn't her fault: it was the role I was willingly playing. I had always been so consumed with whether she liked me, but I never stopped to ask myself if I liked being around her. Our relationship, though mutually beneficial, was not a real friendship.

A few days later, I called Victoria to apologize for ruining the surprise with her sister-in-law. Initially, she acted casual, like she had barely registered the whole incident. But then her voice took on an edge as she admitted that she had been annoyed with me and my actions.

I'm so sorry, I repeated. *For all of it.*

* * *

AFTER THAT NIGHT, Victoria and I started seeing less of each other. She hired an intern, and I stopped getting bags of free clothes. As I started living in a universe without blackouts and hangovers, the lives I had been coveting on Instagram started to feel more distant. I tried to spend less time online and more in the real world.

Influencer culture—and the whole social media landscape—has become our go-to resource for how to live and who to be. Our news feeds are sophisticated algorithms wearing friendly masks, designed to learn about us as consumers while creating the illusion of self-actualization. I write a heartfelt post about a sober milestone, then get served ads for a new line of zero-proof, alcohol-free cocktail mixers. I spend twenty minutes swiping and emerge with one perspective; I am served the one sliver of information that matches my predetermined preferences over and over again.

I'm influenced, therefore I am. Whenever I feel uncomfortable, I go on Instagram. It's a nasty little habit I picked up in the last few years. I scroll for a while, absentmindedly doling out hearts of approval as I peer into other people's lives. Eventually, I come across a post with a promise: a new everyday essential or life hack that someone else swears by. As I read the caption, my heart swells: this new knowledge can become mine to pass on, too, for the low, low price of (fill in the blank, plus 20 percent off with an influencer code). My selfhood crumbles with every click.

I didn't know who I was when I quit drinking, so I looked all around for something, anything, else to fill the empty space. My phone provided immediate assistance. I listened to every voice amplified by a social media platform: I read books, applied lipstick, bought boots, returned boots, listened to podcasts, and ordered herbal supplements. With the right regurgitated opinion or recipe recommendation, I hoped to become a shinier, better me. My identity hung in the hands of the influencers, but my sense of self was in short supply.

As I walked through sobriety, I began to realize that selfhood is not the same as a digital identity. Selfhood was softer, tucked into the quiet questions I asked myself before I fell asleep. I so desperately wanted someone to tell me who I was supposed to be, until it dawned on me that I could just wait and find out. I was still figuring out what I cared about; the causes that mattered to me, and the kind of woman I wanted to become.

There was one positive element I had picked up from Victoria, and it wasn't from her closet. That quiet cool that transformed everything Victoria touched stemmed from a deep well of inner confidence. I had been hoping some of her magic would rub off on me via the transitive property, but it was always an inside job. As I became more comfortable with who I was without alcohol, I dug into my own confidence reserves. I didn't know the name of every trendy clothing brand, but I possessed my own preferences. I had favorite songs, books I treasured, and a journal that only my handwriting filled. I had spent so much time watching other people live through a screen—ordering their coffees, walking their kids to school, doing their hair—that I trusted their recommendations over my own. Social media researchers call this the *compare and despair effect*. But with every day that I practiced being confident, I started to feel more secure in myself. I eyed product recommendations critically. I unsubscribed from newsletters. I stepped away from all the influencers and into the light.

I forgot about the too-small jeans in my closet until a year later, when I was packing up my apartment to move in with my new boyfriend. There, behind sweaters and jackets, was the dusty bag, a single pair of petite designer jeans inside. I held them up, remembering how I had been so willing to trade my sanity to fit into a world that wasn't mine. This life, the one I had built for myself, didn't fit into a phone screen. It was bold and uncomfortable, occasionally messy, and imperfect. It was too big for the smalls, but just right for me.

6

The Pursuit of Wellness

You *have a mustache,* one of the twin boys in my seventh-grade math class informed me. A few of our classmates turned to fact-check his claim, and John or David stared pointedly at my upper lip as if to say, *You're ugly and I can prove it.*

Puberty hit me hard, gracing me with a unibrow, mustache, acne, and braces to bridge the gap between my front teeth that my grandfather told me was lucky. I was wearing a sports bra by fifth grade, the bumps on my chest growing quickly, never giving me a chance to say goodbye to my old body. The other girls in my class were small and soft: they didn't have pimples, hairy upper lips, or breasts. They wore tank tops with tiny spaghetti straps and rolled their Soffe shorts twice, exposing flat strips of stomach.

My mom made me a wax appointment at the fancy

salon in town the day after I came home crying about my mustache. I held my breath as the esthetician slathered hot goo on my lip and told me to relax. The next morning I woke up swollen, the tender skin above my lip angry and inflamed. We had a rule in my house: no fever or vomiting, no sick days. I spent the day at school hiding out in the bathroom, running cold water over brown paper towels, and pressing the makeshift compresses into my face. *My brother punched me in the mouth,* I offered when classmates shot me inquisitive looks. The truth seemed more embarrassing.

I understood immediately that being a girl with facial hair and cystic acne was shameful. I started seeing a dermatologist and having my face poked and prodded. I had extractions, ordered Proactiv products that stained my pillowcases, underwent electrolysis and a botched round of laser treatment, religiously applied topical gels. I averted eye contact in hallways, avoided my reflection in vending machines, and dreamed about what it would feel like to be pretty. *Maybe you should try that,* my dad mentioned offhandedly one night as a Clearasil commercial came on TV. I cried myself to sleep for weeks.

By fifteen, when we had exhausted every other option, my dermatologist prescribed two rounds of Accutane. The potent drug did what nothing had been able to before: clear my acne and give me a taste of the effortless complexion I had always coveted. A month after I finished my final pack of pills, I went to a party, snuck small sips of gin that my crush, Niko, had smuggled into a water bottle from his parents' liquor cabinet, and had my first kiss. The calculation was clear: good skin was a prerequisite for fun, which resulted in attention from the opposite sex.

But it wasn't enough. My arms, I decided one afternoon as I inspected my reflection at the Häagen-Dazs in town, were fat. The word smacked me across the face. *Actually, I told the teenage boy scooping my mint chip cone, I'll have a scoop of sorbet instead.* Dieting, and then restricting, came naturally to me, like a maternal instinct I was born possessing.

Thinking about my appearance all the time was exhausting, and alcohol was the only remedy that helped me tune it all out. I was ashamed of every inch of my body, so I became obsessed with how I could escape and control it.

* * *

THE WELLNESS WORLD ensnared me when I moved to New York City after graduating from college in 2012. Like the alcohol industry, wellness targeted women and swore their products were necessary to achieve our deepest desires. It seemed like boutique fitness studios and juice bars were opening on every city corner, and a new photography app called Instagram was beginning to gain popularity.

I hadn't realized there were so many ways to exercise and eat. In college, I hopped on the elliptical machine a few times a week and snacked on baby carrots and hummus. Now, my friends were filing into spin classes and doing expensive liquid cleanses. Instagram made it easier to discover new workouts and diets; I was introduced to acai bowls and barre workouts, began reading health blogs, and learned what it meant to *eat clean.*

I had been restricting since high school, and my room-mate and I bonded over dieting. For a month we only ate raspberries, spinach, Greek yogurt, and eggs. We woke up hungover and went to the gym together, twin bobble heads on elliptical machines, sweating out last night's vodka so-das before weighing ourselves on the same bathroom scale. I switched to vegan cheese and filled my kitchen cabinets with supplement capsules that made me gag. We upgraded our al-cohol, too, sipping Trader Joe's wine on the couch and swap-ping out sugary mixers like cranberry juice for seltzer when we went out on weekends. Organic wine bars sprouted up around the city and I drank the orange and pink vino like water, genuinely believing it was healthy.

When a friend from college got me a job interview at the hot new plant-based meal delivery service where she worked, I was thrilled. They had a sexy social media presence and my friend raved about the product, expen-sive ready-to-eat meals with superfood ingredients that I could hardly pronounce, let alone afford. In working for the company, she had gained access to the healthy meals that were typically reserved for celebrities and models. She looked thin and I wanted in.

The brand, created by two former models, was hiring for a second full-time employee, an entry-level Operations As-sociate. The co-founders—magnetic twenty-six-year-olds with big Goop energy and older financier boyfriends—seemed to literally glow as they described their vision for a company rooted in holistic health and wellness. At twenty-three, I remember thinking how worldly and wise they both seemed. *Food should be our medicine*, they explained sagely, and I nodded emphatically. I would have done anything they asked; I wanted the glowing complexion and towering height that evidently came from eating plants.

There is a party line that floats around the wellness space: *I struggled with disordered eating once, but now I'm cured.* Veganism, intermittent fasting, juicing, food combining, eating clean, high-protein, low-fat. You name it, there is an evangelist dying to tell you about how it fixed her. These founders told similar stories in interviews, speaking about their past struggles with yo-yo dieting, restrictive fasts, and cystic acne. They had found nirvana in a plant-based diet, and now they were the perfect mix of clean and a little bit bad, posing with romaine lettuce and cocktails. Plant-based eating had changed their lives, and I could be next. I still hated my body and monitored every bite of food I gave it. I would have done anything for freedom that looked this good, and these women were selling it.

I was over the moon when my friend emailed a few days later saying I had gotten the job. *I'm going to be wearing a lot of different hats,* I told my roommate excitedly. I wasn't entirely sure what that meant or what my actual job would entail, but the co-founders had repeated the phrase several times throughout our conversation.

The email did not contain an official offer letter, nor did it have any mention of compensation. When they asked if I could come into the office the following week to sign my papers and begin training, it struck me as a little bit odd that I would be signing my offer letter on the spot, sight unseen. *The founders are at a spiritual retreat in the woods without cell service,* my friend explained when I asked if I could review an offer before starting the job, *but they should be able to get you the paperwork next week. You should also maybe think about if you are going to be comfortable in the startup environment because for better or worse, this is how things run over here.*

I showed up for the training session a few days later. Both founders were still MIA and l had not received a formal offer, but riding the unstructured startup wave felt like a challenge I had to accept, a signal that I was cool and not bothered by unsexy matters like money. (I've made a lot of mistakes in the name of wellness, from drinking laxative teas to going an entire year without eating cheese, but this was one of my silliest.) My friend was eager for me to accept the role—she was clearly overworked and desperate for help—but a knot began to form in my stomach. Was it unrealistic to ask about salary and benefits before accepting a job? (The answer is no.)

Ultimately, when the formal offer letter finally arrived, I was offered a $24,000 annual salary for a full-time Operations Associate role without benefits. My peers were making at least twice as much in their entry-level jobs, and even notoriously underpaid Editorial Assistant roles typically started at $35,000 and included other benefits like healthcare. It was my fault: I had been blinded by the sheen of wellness, the allure of two goddesses promising free salads, the bright light in their co-working space.

I sent back an email apologizing for not asking about salary sooner and explaining that, while I was excited about the company, I simply couldn't make ends meet at that level. *Working for a startup takes a special kind of person and mindset to see the opportunity,* one of the founders responded. *Hopping on with the right startup at the right time offers benefits that go far and beyond monetary compensation. With that said, we wish you the best as you take the next step in your career and hope you find something equally exciting and opportunistic as what we are offering.*

I was ashamed of my naivete, embarrassed, and sad that I would be relegated to eating boring food for normal people again. As the company grew, they hired a small army of recent college graduates who wore crop tops that revealed their flat stomachs. I wondered how they all afforded to pay rent, book workout classes, and buy new clothes. Living off a low salary, I thought, required an inherent smallness, a delicate, mouse-like ability to eat half now and save the rest for later. The secret no one talked about was that many of these employees had outside help paying their bills. To be clear, my family provided me with financial and emotional support as a young adult navigating life in New York, and I possessed a significant amount of privilege as a white, college-educated woman who walked away from one job offer confident that she would receive another. But this new world seemed to exist beyond a line I was able to cross. So I remained on the outskirts of the sexy sorority known as the wellness industry.

* * *

SIX YEARS LATER, I accepted a VP of Marketing position at a different New York wellness brand. This time, I was offered a competitive salary with benefits and stock options. I was a little over a year sober and had just exited another startup with a work-hard, play-hard culture. In this new role, I would manage a team, oversee a rebranding, and work directly with the founder, a petite Brooklyn mom in her thirties.

Perhaps more significantly, the position gave me access to the underbelly of the wellness world, which had continued to evolve since initially piquing my interest years earlier. I learned more about this subculture as I started attending industry events with vague titles like Health & Wellness Summit, Glow from Within Wellness Breakfast, and the Annual Wellness Awards. These gatherings were identical: a room of women in flowy dresses and designer jeans held half-empty plates of photogenic "bites" (purple sweet potato toast with tahini and edible flowers, anyone?) until some sort of panel began.

In the beginning, I was thrilled to be attending these insider events. I eagerly dressed the part, snapping selfies of myself surrounded by swag samples like jade rollers, bottles of juices, adaptogenic teas, and *gua sha* face stones. I felt invigorated and in good company. Finally, fulfillment was within reach, the angular body and dewy complexion of my dreams at my fingertips. All I had to do was consume what these women were selling. But these informational sessions merely provided a front row seat to the whiplash of wellness trends.

The rules were always changing. Oat milk, I learned, was now enemy number one. (Too much sugar.) Bakuchiol was the new retinol. Intermittent fasting could have a negative impact on your hormones, but a positive impact on your energy. Coffee was bad unless it was bulletproofed with Brain Octane C8 MCT oil and ghee. Matcha was so five years ago, unless you were mixing it with adaptogens, probiotics, and superfoods. Even water was insufficient; instead, there was rose water, beauty drops, CBD water. Weight loss was usually implied, but brands and panelists spoke in euphemisms instead. *Less stress, better digestion, deeper sleep, higher energy levels, clearer skin.*

At these events, my inner child stirred. I felt like the girl in class with the mustache again, and I was willing to buy and do whatever the cool girls told me would make me pretty. I wanted to be skinny, fresh faced, and accepted. Still, I was confused. Now that I was sober, my brain was slowly clearing from my former alcohol-induced haze. I was becoming increasingly aware that every time I bought one product, there was a new one waiting to rebuke it. I spent my salary on serums, creams, masks, and cleansers. I spun, stretched, took probiotics, waxed, and exfoliated. I ate superfoods, logged my water intake, and counted my steps. My pursuit of wellness was exhausting, time-consuming, and expensive. But the stakes felt too high to walk away, especially now that I wasn't partying anymore. This was my chance to *glow*. I needed to unlock the life-changing serenity people described finding in their superfoods and skincare products.

One winter night, I took the subway from Brooklyn to the Upper East Side for a wellness talk that my boss asked me to attend. The event was being hosted at a private residence on a quiet, brownstone-lined street just off Park Avenue. I followed the map on my cracked phone screen to the last house on the block, an impressive corner building with three floors. When I buzzed the door, a woman immediately ushered me inside and took my coat. As I checked my reflection in the foyer's opulent mirror, I regretted wearing an old pair of jeans.

I made my way into the living room where several women in their thirties and forties were eyeing a table of vegan hors d'oeuvres. Expensive art hung from the walls, and all the furniture in the room had been arranged to form a semicircle. I perched on a white couch, too nervous to put any food on my plate. I worried I would spill something, or worse, chew too loudly in a roomful of nibblers.

In the center of the room, a beautiful woman sat very still. I recognized her from the website I had skimmed on my way uptown; she was the speaker at this event and the author of a new book about how to determine the best diet for your body type. After the author described her approach to wellness and the quiz she had created for people to understand their ideal diets, the guests in the room were encouraged to ask questions.

A petite woman stood up and began to speak. She was frustrated: she ate an extremely healthy diet and worked out every day, but she couldn't seem to lose the weight from her upper arms. I blinked. Her arms were toned and fit, without an ounce of excess fat. I pulled my sleeves down, hoping to hide my own arms. If hers were fat, what were mine?

The author nodded at the woman knowingly. *You must*

be a nurturer, she said easily. *Upper arm fat can be very hard for nurturers to lose. It's because you spend so much time caring for and carrying others.* She emphasized the last two words. *When you're caring for everyone else, it can set you up for comfort eating, which leads to estrogen dominance. So, start doing less for them and more for you. You'll lose the arm fat.* The author seemed satisfied and began to scan the room, looking for the next raised hand. But the petite woman with invisible arm fat wasn't finished yet. *But what does that mean? What workouts should I do? What should I eat?*

There was an edge to her voice, a ring of panic. From the outside, she was a picture of perfection: the massive engagement ring and diamond wedding band, expensive clothes, highlighted hair, manicured nails. She referenced a loving husband and beautiful children and belonged to the kind of exclusive social circle that nonchalantly hosted authors at their homes for intimate chats. But she was still convinced her body wasn't good enough.

I looked around, confused. The rest of the women were staring at the author eagerly, waiting to hear her answer. Every single one of them was glowing, fit, and healthy, and yet they were all searching for the next product and magic solution.

I recognized the hope on their faces as they waited for the author to speak. Whenever I bought a new beauty product or supplement, I got high on the same strain of hope. This, I always thought, would finally fix me. *This moisturizer changed my life,* every online review read, and I believed it every time.

Stick to lots of leafy vegetables and lean protein, the author finally said unhelpfully. *And remember that when you do ev-erything for everyone, it can set you up for sugar cravings.*

As I left the event an hour later, my stomach rumbled. I was starving, I realized. Not just for food, but for some-thing more satiating than conversations about optimizing digestion and losing arm fat. I had spent the better part of my life striving to be anything other than what I was. I drank to escape my body, and now that I was sober, I was still trying to change it.

I wanted a body that was lean, long, thin, fit, active, strong, fast, tight, tucked, and skin that was plump, glow-ing, bouncy, dewy, and hydrated. Like my drinking, it was all too much and never enough. I was bottoming out on wellness, I realized. But I wasn't sure I was ready to walk away from it. Wellness had been a pleasant distraction and safe catch-all for my feelings for the better part of a de-cade. Whenever I felt angry, hurt, or sad, I focused on my weight instead of digging into the root of my feelings. I had wrapped my identity around drinking and changing my body, and I wondered what would be left of me if I unraveled this thread too.

As I contemplated this, I found myself marching past Park Avenue and onto Lexington. I walked for blocks until I found a pizza parlor on the corner. The smell was warm and inviting, and for the first time, I let myself breathe it in. I usually only indulged in dollar slices when I was drunk or hungover, as a cheesy remedy or treat. This was my first time soberly ordering myself a slice. On my way out of the restaurant, I inhaled deeply and took a huge bite. The pizza was still hot, and the bubbling cheese burnt the roof of my mouth. For days, I rubbed my tongue over the burn, smiling to myself with the memory of what it felt like to honor my hunger.

* * *

I ONCE READ a magazine article about what a supermodel ate in a day. KIND Bars were her favorite healthy snack, and on busy days she would have one half of the bar in the morning and the second half later in the afternoon. I have remembered this anecdote for my entire adult life, swallowing shame every time I finish a KIND Bar in one sitting.

After that night on the Upper East Side, extracting myself from the world of wellness took time. For starters, I still had my job. But over the next few months, it became increasingly clear that my heart simply wasn't in the wellness business. When I left the company a few months later, I was hungry for something different. I thought about the paltry job offer I had walked away from years earlier, the shame I had felt when I admitted that I wanted more. Now, for the first time in my life, my hunger didn't scare me.

I needed to begin the process of unlearning everything I had spent years cramming into my brain about what it meant to be healthy. The very fact that I was sober meant that I was taking better care of myself than ever before. I was sleeping more, eating three normal meals a day, and not bingeing on greasy food after a night of partying. Maybe that was enough.

I also began to think critically about my relationship with wellness and alcohol. My quest for nirvana through wellness had not been unlike my pursuit of drunkenness. I thought of both as elixirs that could fix me quickly, and with little real work on my part. I would have bought anything the wellness industry told me would make me glow, strut, and sleep better. Similarly, alcohol touted a promise of ease, relaxation, and confidence. Both worlds promoted the idea of balance (*Drink responsibly!*) while shirking any real responsibility for outcomes (*Consult a doctor before beginning a new fitness regimen!*). There's no time for consultations or responsible consumption when you're trying to change everything about yourself.

Through abstaining from drinking, I began to clean up the wreckage from my drunken nights and simplify my life. All the parties, bars, and drinks had been like clutter in my brain. As the mess cleared, I was able to take steps toward actual balance.

The same applied to my wellness journey. I had spent so much time and money trying to *figure out* the right way to eat, exercise, and take care of my skin. But it wasn't working: I had hit my wellness bottom. So I pared down my routine, asked for help, and began to work on my gut health. Not the probiotic kind; the intuition kind. I started eating fruit even though bloggers said it had too much sugar. I stopped booking overpriced workout classes that I hated. I made an appointment with a licensed esthetician and asked questions about serums.

I heard people in my recovery meetings say that hitting

bottom doesn't have to be catastrophic; it can simply mean that we are ready to stop digging. I was ready to stop living in my wellness hole. But this meant admitting something I had never said out loud before: in my world, *wellness* had just been a fancy word for diet. Underneath the gloss of new products and promises, all I had ever wanted was to be small, and look like all the other girls.

But I wasn't like every other girl. For the first time in my life, I was stepping into what it meant to just be me. I wondered what my life might look like, what I might look like, if I took all the brain space I had devoted to drinking and dieting since I was a teenager and refocused it elsewhere: on writing or reading or traveling or being a better daughter, sister, and friend. It seemed like anything was possible, and I found myself feeling high on hope. But this time, the spark didn't require any fancy juices, wellness powders, supplements, pills, or meal plans. It came from me.

7

Seduced by Startup Culture

On graduation day, we all woke up to a tragedy.

Marina Keegan, who had graduated from Yale University five days earlier, died in a car accident on Cape Cod. The news spread quickly, sobering us up as we rolled over and checked our phones. Brown and Yale were a short train ride apart, and Marina visited campus often. I had seen her a handful of times—in the dining hall, at a friend's off-campus house—but in typical twenty-something fashion, she was my friend's ex-boyfriend's current girlfriend, so I stayed away. The last time I saw her, a month before her death, I caught a flash of her sleeve as she closed the door to a friend's bedroom.

This is all to say that we were hardly acquaintances, let alone close friends. We didn't even follow each other on social media. But Marina's death had an impact on me. A few weeks before she passed away, Marina penned an essay entitled "The Opposite of Loneliness" for *Yale Daily News. We don't have a word for the opposite of loneliness,* Marina wrote, *but if we did, I could say that's what I want in life. What I'm grateful and thankful to have found at Yale, and what I'm scared of losing when we wake up tomorrow and leave this place.*

Marina put words to the feelings I had been binge drinking to conceal. My boyfriend, Jack, and I had broken up one week earlier, and I had been walking around in a blackout ever since, postponing the inevitable pain I knew was coming. I was terrified about the transition in front of me, the chasm stretching between the life I knew and my future. My friends were all ready to leap into their next adventures: law school, Teach For America, consulting jobs. I had dreamed about moving to New York and working in magazines, starting out as an Editorial Assistant before working my way up the ranks to Editor. But despite my Creative Writing degree and internship experience, I struggled to nab the jobs a million other girls had apparently already killed for. I made it to the final interview for an assistant role at a food magazine but missed a typo in a copy-editing test that cost me the job. (The second *A* in Rachael Ray still haunts me.)

I pivoted to my backup plan: finding literally any entry-level job so I could move to New York City with Jack. Yes, we had spent the first half of senior year broken up and hating each other, but none of that mattered now. We were back together and in the kind of toxic relationship that convinces you love is supposed to hurt this much. We spent that spring smoking pot and applying for random jobs. I fell asleep at night tangled in his sheets, high enough to ignore the nagging feeling that something wasn't right.

I hadn't spent a single night alone in the past three years; I was either in Jack's bed or crashing on friends' couches. Our campus was a cocoon, protecting me from the outside world. My biggest decision was whether to register for a morning class on Fridays (no) or skip a party to study (also no). Moving to New York with Jack would be like a sitcom: I imagined us meeting friends at our neighborhood bar, spending Sundays in Central Park, brunching at our favorite greasy spoon diner.

But our flimsy foundation was ripped out from under me when Jack drunkenly told me I had gotten fat a few days before graduation. His words were the cruelest he could think of, he explained in an email years later, his last-ditch attempt at sabotaging a relationship that had become too serious for college seniors.

On graduation day, I was confronted by the creeping realization that I had no idea who I was or what I wanted. My identity had been so wrapped up in being Jack's girlfriend, and my heartbreak was mixed with fear. *What doesn't kill you makes you stronger,* Kelly Clarkson had promised at every party that spring, but I wasn't sure. I clung to my friends, retelling my breakup story, attending every party, falling asleep midsentence, keeping everyone close so that I wouldn't have to spend a second by myself.

I read Marina's essay the night we found out she died, a few hours after receiving my diploma. When she wrote about the future, it felt like she was speaking directly to me. *We won't live on the same block as all our friends. We won't have a bunch of group texts. This scares me. More than finding the right job or city or spouse—I'm scared of losing this web we're in. This elusive, indefinable, opposite of loneliness.*

My sadness turned to shame. I was struck by the envy I felt as I read Marina's words. She was a talented and dedicated writer who had managed to produce an entire book of work by the age of twenty-two. I said I wanted to be a writer but was usually too hungover and worried about what people thought of me to write anything worth noticing. Marina wrote with passion, a deep conviction in who she was and what she believed. I felt numb, clunky, insecure in comparison. But her writing also moved me. I was inspired by her ability to own and articulate her feelings. Like Marina, I was twenty-two and scared of losing my place in the world. I didn't know her well enough to grieve for her, and yet I read every Facebook post and news story about her accident. I was disgusted by myself as I went to therapy, laid on my couch, and cried about Jack. I had the opportunity to do everything Marina couldn't: write, laugh, fall in love again. And yet I just felt empty, barely treading water until New York swallowed me up whole.

* * *

IN 2016, WHEN Barack Obama was finishing his term as president and I was obsessed with Lin-Manuel Miranda, I got a new job. I had spent the last four years bouncing between jobs, studying for various graduate school entrance exams, working at a fitness studio, and going out in the city. I pulled myself together enough to enroll in a part-time MFA program in Creative Writing in New York, but I was distracted. I felt aimless, untethered to a real community, desperate for change.

A few years earlier, three of my college classmates had founded Casper, a mattress company that everybody was talking about. The business reported $100 million in sales within its first year of operations, but I was more interested in its culture. Social media depicted cute employees in their twenties and thirties attending regular happy hours and smiling brightly. I had struggled to find my place in the corporate world, fielding panic attacks in the bathroom of my first marketing job and scrolling through LinkedIn job listings like a dating app. Startups, it seemed, offered a less constricting way to work. If you were intelligent and ambitious, you could skip paying your dues and cut ahead to vague and ubiquitous job titles like Customer Experience Lead, Head of Partnerships, or Brand Director. Working at a startup also offered sexy perks like beer and kombucha on tap, an inflated sense of importance, and a close-knit circle of coworkers your own age.

I looked out west, applying for a handful of jobs in San Francisco and Silicon Valley, before receiving an offer in an equally exotic locale: Brooklyn. I would be the first full-time employee at an early-stage tech startup, which meant I wouldn't have health insurance but would work for two founders in their late twenties. They interviewed me in a hotel lobby in Williamsburg, and I immediately found them fascinating; Andrew, a curly haired man wearing skinny jeans and wire frame glasses, was the CEO and brains behind the operation. He described himself as a lifelong entrepreneur and talked about his lofty aspirations for the brand. The other founder, Clark, a former standup comedian who towered over me when I shook his hand, was friendly and talkative. He would change his title several times over the next few years, but on that day, he introduced himself as Head of Business Development. I knew the moment I left that interview that two friends in their late twenties who had just raised $2 million in venture capital funding were going to become key characters in my life.

There are different ways to tell the rest of this story, various threads to flesh out when dissecting how a job becomes your entire life. First, there is the energy of a startup: the evangelical look in a founder's eye when he tells you why his idea is going to change the world. Startup founders would make excellent cult leaders; it takes a certain kind of charisma and self-confidence to convince an army of people to buy into your vision. As an employee, a mission statement gets drilled into your head repeatedly over time until one night you find yourself slightly brainwashed and rattling it off to friends who don't care. As the first hire, my role encompassed a slew of responsibilities, from answering customer service emails and packing boxes to copywriting and planning events. In time, the founders began referring to me as the keeper of our brand voice, a title I found exhilaratingly important. There was so much work to do in building something from scratch, and I felt a dizzying sense of possibility and pride. I was twenty-five, and being part of something so much bigger than me was intoxicating.

Next, there are the social dynamics. The more time you spend with your coworkers, the more convinced you become that your job is the center of the world. Both founders told me I was building this brand with them, that I could have any job title I wanted down the line, that I had gotten in on something big at the ground level. Their passion was contagious; I convinced myself that their dreams were mine. I updated my own Instagram profile to include the company's handle and started spending time with the founders outside the office, listening intently as they retold the story of how they launched the business. The job, and brand, slowly started to become an extension of my personality. The founders and I spent late nights at the office and bonded quickly, like kids at sleepaway camp. We ate meals together, attended each other's birthday parties, and celebrated milestones like Clark's engagement to his longtime girlfriend, a social media influencer. Being a part of their lives made me feel special, like I had finally found the kind of community I had been craving since my college graduation. Clark was the funny one; Andrew was the one I wanted to impress.

Finally, there is the Kool-Aid. I drank it all, every drop, but was still thirsty for more. We were going to make waves, the founders said, reinvent the market, disrupt the industry, be the change we wished to see. Andrew and Clark carried themselves with the confidence of two men who, despite little formal work experience, had always been "cool." There was no imposter syndrome or crisis of confidence; they were used to commanding whatever room they entered. Andrew was whip smart and showed up to investor meetings on a skateboard carrying a vintage briefcase. Clark told jokes and led with the brand's origin story. People were intrigued by the duo, never quite knowing what to make of them. I came to trust them deeply.

We don't have a word for the opposite of loneliness, Marina wrote in her last essay for *Yale Daily News, but if we did, I'd say that's how I feel at Yale. How I feel right now. Here. With all of you. In love, impressed, humbled, scared.*

In the fold of my startup, I remembered Marina's words. Being happy at work, discovering a sense of purpose, and finding a community was the opposite of the loneliness I had been wading through since moving to New York. Meeting friends for the occasional dinner or night out was nice, but it didn't provide the deep sense of satisfaction I found at work. I finally felt like I had found my place, and I didn't ever want to go back.

* * *

IT WAS CLEAR from the beginning that the founders wanted to create something big. *One day, when we have five hundred employees, you'll be able to say you were the first,* Clark said to me one night over empanadas in Brooklyn, a couple of blocks away from our new office space. I had been working with them for about five months, and we had recently rented out the back room of an art library in East Williamsburg, a dimly lit space that came with two long tables, a small couch, and a finicky heater. We took meetings at a restaurant around the corner, ignoring the glares from the waitstaff when we used their free WiFi but didn't order food. From the outside, it probably looked like we could barely afford to keep the lights on. But Andrew and Clark had their sights set on greatness; they talked about the business like it was already bringing in millions of dollars. I never said it out loud, but the thought of ballooning to a company of five hundred people overnight terrified me. I didn't want to lose the tight-knit community and sense of belonging I had finally uncovered.

Still, I knew we needed to hire more people. I was slogging through customer service emails, struggling to stay afloat in a sea of complaints. I needed help, but I worried I would feel less important if I had less work to do.

You'll be able to do anything you want in a couple of months, Andrew promised one afternoon as we shared a chocolate chip cookie during our weekly one-on-one meeting. I knew he was trying to motivate me to hold on until we could build a dedicated customer service team. I had heard the speech before, usually when I was expressing my frustration at being expected to answer customer emails at nights and on weekends. This was temporary, he always promised. Once we brought on additional pairs of hands, I could work on what excited me most.

But what excited me most was his belief in me: *you can do anything.* He believed in my talent as a writer, trusted me to tell the brand story across different channels, and brainstormed with me when he had an idea. His eyes lit up when he spoke; it was exciting that someone so charismatic and intelligent had faith in me.

I began to give Andrew an outlandish amount of power. I craved his praise and validation, wanted him to give me a gold star and pat on the head for the smallest tasks. I felt buoyant every time he sent me a Slack message asking if I wanted to split lunch. I soared when he gave me a copy of apartment keys, even if it was only so I could dog sit for him. Can you watch Ollie this weekend? He would text me on a Friday. You're the only one he trusts. I loved his dog, but it hadn't occurred to me that I might have feelings for him too. Then, after seeing us walking home from work together one night, a friend who also lived in the neighborhood texted me: Who is the guy?! I saw serious sparks. It gave me chills!

It was like being hit upside the head. *Do I . . . love him?* I asked my roommate. I told myself it was an innocent crush, but the weight of my feelings became much more confusing with time. Andrew was my boss, the person I spent the most time with, and someone I admired. We were close in age, lived a block apart, and ran into each other at coffee shops and restaurants. He was everywhere, all the time. After work, when he and I split a bottle of wine at dinner and walked home together, I felt like a teenager. When he hugged me goodnight, I held on a little too long.

Both founders described themselves as my friends (*We're not just coworkers; we're a family,* they repeated) and I believed them, ignoring the tiny voice in my head reminding me that they signed my paychecks. We drank together regularly, implementing team happy hours and drinking beer and wine on late nights in the office. We joked about our hangovers, and Andrew ordered Pedialyte to the office as a cure. Because of our friendships outside of work, I began to feel overly comfortable with Andrew and Clark. Our shared lack of professional boundaries created a strange dynamic where we confided in each other, kept secrets, and butted heads. I forgot they were my bosses, and when work issues arose, I struggled to manage my reactions.

One night, I met Andrew and Clark at a club in Manhattan. They were celebrating a birthday and drinks were flowing. Whiskey, palomas, tequila. Everyone moved onto the dance floor, and I stood off to the side, waiting for the bartender to finish making my drink. When I turned around, Andrew was making out with a girl. I felt a mix of embarrassment, jealousy, and stupidity. I knew there was nothing real between us, but for some reason it hurt to see him being intimate with someone else.

It was important to the founders that I feel equally invested in the company; they reminded me often that we were building it together. *Titles don't matter,* they routinely shrugged whenever I asked questions about where I sat in the organization. Their intentions weren't malicious. It felt more like they just weren't sure what to do with me yet, this girl who was utterly willing to attach her sail to theirs and devote her life to executing their vision.

Being the only woman in the office could be challenging. On the day after Donald Trump won the presidential election of 2016, I walked into work feeling like a zombie.

I had started watching coverage the night before at a bar with Andrew and Clark and stayed up late watching the final results in disbelief. That morning, Brooklyn had a gray, somber quality; I passed women crying on the sidewalk, and we exchanged uneasy eye contact. It felt like everything had shifted. How could a man with such blatant disregard for the female body have been elected president? At work, Andrew and Clark seemed unbothered. *He's a solid businessman,* Clark said. *I think he'll do a good job.* I smiled tightly and nodded.

When a male investor came to visit the office that fall, he shook hands with Andrew and a new employee, a recent college graduate named Rob. The three of them chatted like old friends while I worked at the same table. We were the only four people in the room, but the investor sat in the seat right next to mine with his back to me for over an hour. He never made eye contact or said hello. *We need to get some more hot girls in here,* he joked at one point as Andrew shifted in his seat and avoided my eyes. When the investor left, I was close to tears. I felt humiliated, invisible in a room of men, foolish for believing I might actually have a seat at the table.

That kind of shit happens all the time at startups. They have no idea what they're doing, my roommate Nina told me that night as I recounted the story. *Just remember that you can never let them see you cry.*

But I did. I broke the cardinal rule at work: I showed them my cards, my emotions written all over my face whenever I was disappointed or frustrated. Andrew told me to never stop caring as much as I did, that my passion was an asset to the company. But I cared too much. About the company, about my job, about him. And I hated myself for it.

This is your career, I reminded myself calmly as I got dressed for work every morning. *Having a crush on your boss is the exact opposite of what you're supposed to do as a strong woman at work. So just let it go. You barely like him, anyway.* I repeated this monologue as I drank my coffee, walked to the office, and sat at my desk. But by the end of the day, my inner voice was desperate and defeated. *Do not go to dinner with him. No, you're not free tonight. Close your laptop and say goodnight. Okay, fine. But just one drink.* I tried everything to squash my feelings, but the boundaries were always getting blurry. I would go to lunch without him, and he would pick up on my energy, sending me a message asking if everything was okay. We had intense debates over customer service replies and social media copy, our heated exchanges escalating until I couldn't even remember what we were arguing about. At times our rapport was exhilarating, pushing us both to think critically. In other moments it was exhausting, a strange dynamic that Clark watched from the outside. Sometimes I behaved poorly, like a sullen child. *You angry?* Andrew texted when I left the office without saying goodbye to him. He was attuned to my moods, could sense when I was upset about something, and always pressed me about what was on my mind.

Our connection was bewildering. On some days I felt like I knew where we stood: boss and coworker, something adjacent to friends. In other moments, like when he leaned over my shoulder to type something on my laptop or touched my arm after everyone else had already gone home for the night, I felt my heartbeat quicken and cursed my feelings. I knew, deep down, that I wanted so much more from him. In some moments I felt sure that he knew how I felt; in others I was positive he was completely oblivious. It didn't matter. In either scenario, I knew neither of us would cross the ultimate line.

Forgive me, Andrew texted me the night before Yom Kippur, the Day of Atonement in the Jewish faith.

For? The year?

And beyond, he responded quickly.

I forgive you. I thought about all the office arguments, the times I had cried in the bathroom. Forgive me?

I forgive you.

I thought it would be our fresh start. But I didn't know then how much worse everything was about to get.

* * *

A LITTLE OVER a year after I joined the startup, the company started to grow. We raised more venture capital funding and Andrew and Clark began hiring rapidly. We doubled in size within a month, and our office began to feel crowded. Trash piled in the kitchen, and we routinely ran out of toilet paper. We hired an office manager and rented out the basement floor of our Brooklyn building to accommodate more desks. Several new employees were hired and fired quickly for creative differences with Andrew and Clark, and I became terrified of being replaced and losing my spot at the company. Andrew and Clark started spending more time in Andrew's new office, the door closed behind them. I worked hard but could never tell if they were happy with my performance. I clung to my responsibilities tightly, fear and insecurity dominating my thoughts.

Alcohol became more entrenched in every aspect of my job: I drank to keep up, to seem cool around coworkers, to hide my feelings for Andrew, and to cope with the new emotions creeping up at work. My identity was enmeshed with the startup, and as more people started to join, I felt my grip slipping. When I wasn't working, I was drinking and thinking about work. I tried dating, but the men I went out with typically lost interest when I spent the entire night talking about why my company was going to change the world. My hangovers felt thick and heavy, but I still showed up to work early, a nitro cold brew sweating on my desk by the time the rest of the office arrived. My title was often changing, my role a mishmash of marketing and administrative responsibilities that changed week to week. One week, I was managing two direct reports. The next, Andrew and Clark were hiring someone new to run our team. The energy in the office began to feel chaotic and unpredictable, and when I walked past Clark's desk, I often saw him scrolling through LinkedIn, searching for talent to poach. A new hire pulled me aside at happy hour to ask if Andrew and I were secretly dating, and I laughed a little too loudly. *Why would you ask that?* I replied, hoping I didn't sound overeager. *He's just always with you or looking for you.* She shrugged, already bored by the conversation. When I saw a copy of a new organizational chart Andrew had made, I was hurt to see that there was a question mark next to my name where everyone else had titles. I hated him; I loved him. I wished I could muster the kind of faith the founders routinely begged me to channel; I had believed in them so deeply when this all started. But I began having nightmares about being fired. If they hired someone else, where would that leave me?

The last time I ever drank was with Andrew. It was a Friday night, and we had dinner at his apartment with his roommate and his roommate's girlfriend. Andrew served steak and red wine. *Is this a double date?* I wondered for half a second. *No way; you're his employee. He definitely thinks you're gross.* I drank more wine and took what I hoped were very ladylike bites of steak. After dinner, Andrew's friends arrived and started passing around a bottle of whiskey. Andrew went into his bedroom with a girl, and my heart sank. I knew I should leave, but I kept drinking. *So what if he doesn't like me in that way? At least I can keep up and show him how fun I am.* A few drinks later, my memory of the night ended.

The next morning, I woke up naked next to one of his friends. I had no memory of what had happened between us. The shame was blinding. I threw up in the friend's bathroom and walked home wearing my clothes from the night before. I spent the next forty-eight hours lying on my couch, wondering what had happened to my body and praying Andrew wouldn't hold it against me. On Monday morning, we both acted like nothing had happened.

It wasn't the first time I had woken up in a strange place, but I finally hated myself enough to accept what it meant: I was done drinking.

Two things changed after I got sober: I clung to my job even tighter, and a new woman started working at my company. She was a couple of years older than me and had previously worked at a successful startup. Andrew hung on her every word, and the two of them began spending a lot of time together. He started rescheduling our meetings and walking past my desk at lunchtime, sharing sandwiches with her instead. The new girl had an intense energy and was a self-described *guy's girl.*

Her first order of business was planning a full-blown office holiday party with a DJ and bartender. *It's going to be lit,* she repeated in the weeks leading up to it, encouraging the founders to drink freely and give the rest of the team permission to let loose. I didn't tell anyone at work that I had stopped drinking. But I began to panic as the party approached, especially when I learned that Andrew had asked his friend—the one I had woken up next to three months earlier—to DJ the party. *I haven't seen you out in a while,* his friend said when he greeted me, and my stomach turned.

The new girl passed around a tray of shots, pushing everyone to drink more. I avoided her eyes as I excused myself, only returning from the bathroom when I was sure everyone had finished their shots.

I'm struggling so much with work stuff, I wrote in my journal a few nights later. *I feel like no one has any idea what they're doing, but we just keep hiring more people. People keep telling me I should quit, but I can't imagine working anywhere else. I have such anxiety. I'm so obsessed with the need for validation, praise, and a better title. I cried in the bathroom today and I feel really lost. Is it always going to feel like this?*

As I began attending recovery meetings, I started to notice a shift in my attitude toward work. I swore I still loved it, but for the first time in almost two years I started to detach from the intense social component of my job. I began to leave the office at 7:00 PM instead of hanging around and waiting to see if Andrew would ask me to get drinks or dinner. He had grown disinterested in me, anyway, walking past my desk silently when he left the office, and saying nothing on my birthday. His new indifference hurt—I wasn't sure what had changed for him—but it was also a gift. I started spending time with other friends and remembering the interests I used to have before the startup.

One Friday night after work when I was eleven months sober, I went to a yoga class near my apartment. At the end of the hour, as I lay on my mat, I started to write an essay in my head. The words flowed naturally, an idea taking shape as my body remained still.

I had taken a leave of absence from my part-time MFA program a few months into working at the startup, a decision Andrew and Clark reassured me was the right one for my career. I had never regretted not finishing my program; work had been exciting, fun, and all-consuming for the last two years. But now, as my brain cleared without alcohol, I realized I missed writing for myself.

When I got home from yoga that night, I sat down

at my computer and started to type. I composed a three-paragraph pitch that I emailed to an editor at my favorite magazine. There was no outside voice promising me that I would succeed at this, but I heard a quiet inner voice encouraging me to try anyway.

Two days later, I woke up and found a response from the editor accepting my story idea. I worked on the essay before work and on weekends, and when my story was published a month later, I shared it on social media. I had never felt more proud—or nervous.

The story was about my recent experiences dating without alcohol, and most people still didn't know I was sober. *When I quit drinking last fall, I was scared to tell my closest friends, let alone share about it on social media,* I wrote on Instagram when I posted the piece. *But this Sunday marks one year sober . . . So excited (and a little bit terrified) to share one part of my story today.* Andrew and Clark never said anything to me about the essay, though a coworker told me she saw Clark reading it on his computer at work.

As Andrew and Clark stepped further into their identities as founders of a growing company and I discovered who I was without alcohol, the framework of our dynamic began to crumble. I realized that my obsession with work had been another form of escape, like my drinking. I genuinely loved the startup and was so proud of the work I had done there, but I was also changing. Still, I never seriously considered leaving the company; I was in too deep to see any way out. But the founders made the decision for me.

One day, during our regular weekly catch-up meeting,

Clark began to direct the conversation away from work. He said it seemed like I had been distracted recently; I wasn't attending as many happy hours, and my heart didn't seem to be in the brand anymore. When I asked if my work was suffering, he assured me that my performance was fine. Still, over the course of an hourlong talk, I kept feeling like he was trying to convince me to quit. At the end of the meeting, he said it would be best if I left the office for the day. I called my dad on my walk home, confused and in tears. *Did he just fire me?*

I emailed Clark and Andrew and asked if we could talk. *I've been reflecting on the conversation we had today and I'm feeling extremely confused about it . . . I don't really understand whether you were trying to give me career advice and suggesting that I reflect on whether this is the right long-term opportunity for me or firing me on the spot without any notice or cause,* I wrote. We scheduled time to meet for coffee the next day, but I knew as soon as I saw them that they had made their decision. *We've felt a strain in our relationships,* Andrew and Clark announced. There were no issues with my work performance, no two-week notice, but they believed my time at the company had come to an end. As an at-will employee, I was not entitled to a formal review and notice, so the conversation ended there.

It was true I wasn't happy with them; they weren't the same people I had met two years earlier. But I was stunned when they asked me not to return to the office or talk to any of my coworkers again. I thought of all the unfinished projects, the pink mug still sitting on my desk (*I Am Woman,*

Hear Me Roar, a silly gift from Andrew). I remembered all the other employees who had been there one day and mysteriously disappeared the next. I had feared becoming one of them, a leper the rest of the team was taught to pity. I wept as I walked home from the coffee shop, unable to believe this was the end.

And yet, on the other side of the startup, I found freedom. In my recovery meetings, I began to discover a deep sense of community that wasn't contingent on job performance or who had worked at a trendy company before. And I started to unpack some of the reasons I had clutched my work life so tightly in the first place.

When you don't know who you are, your job can be an excellent placeholder. This is perhaps most pervasive among the twenty- and thirty-something set who still don't have families of their own and are freefalling through cities, lost and searching for a broader purpose. For many, the Instagram bio becomes a digital calling card: in tagging where you work, your brand becomes an extension of your personality. My job title was who I was, the first and most impressive trait I wanted people to see when they found my online profile. But there is a difference between using social media to brand yourself as a professional and attaching yourself to a larger institution because you don't know who you are without it.

On the alcohol front, there is nothing inherently wrong with drinking at work functions. Coworkers have been drinking together since the days of yore. Cavemen brewed ale and grunted about their bosses, while farmers drank beer made from barley after sowing the fields. Okay, so maybe none of that is historically accurate. But studies do show that human ancestors began consuming alcohol as early as ten million years ago, which is a whole lot of co-workers ago. It makes sense: workplace dynamics can be stressful, and drinking is a great way to blow off steam and bond with the stranger who sits next to you all day. There is also a very real fear of missing out on professional opportunities and team bonding if you skip drinks.

But I was *that girl* at work: I brought balloons for people's birthdays and was the last one to leave every office party. It was all too much, and I doubt any of it was making me look incredibly professional. I simply clung to it because I thought I needed it. Losing that job was one of the best things that ever happened to me because it freed me from my limiting beliefs about myself. Getting along with coworkers is one thing; attaching your self-worth to your company and bosses is trickier. I learned this lesson the hard way.

My world revolved around my company because I let it. I didn't have the confidence to cultivate interests outside of work, so I became a supporting character in my own life, casting Andrew as the lead. I had feelings for someone who was emotionally unavailable because it was all I thought I was worth. And as afraid as I had once been to lose the startup, letting it go brought me more than I could have ever imagined. The opposite of loneliness, I wish I could tell Marina now, is finding people with whom you can be your most authentic self. I didn't end up finding them at work, but I did meet them eventually. It just took me a little bit longer to believe I deserved them.

8

Flirtini

My senior year of college, an old building was renovated on campus. During the day, the walkways were blocked off with sunny tape. But in the early hours of morning, students found a way to infiltrate. It went like this: after the bars closed at 2:00 AM and the rest of campus tucked itself into a velvety blanket of beer, the academic quad sat still, prim, and fastidious. In these quiet hours, campus felt like my own. I traced the storied brick buildings with my eyes, imagining all the lost hearts that had walked these lawns before me.

If you walked too fast, you missed it: the ladder hanging off the side of the old Psychology building. At five-foot-four, I needed to be hoisted onto a taller pair of shoulders to pull down the base of the ladder until it hovered just above the ground. From there, I shimmied myself up the side of the building, belly flopping onto the roof like a fish. The view of the adjacent library was mediocre at best, but there was something vaguely romantic about the taboo sliver of dark sky.

When these renovations started, I was on a break with Jack, my college beau. I spent that fall semester getting too drunk at parties and kissing boys I convinced myself I cared about, hoping I would eventually forget the one who still had my heart. On late nights, after the bars closed and the pizza parlor ran out of dollar slices, I took these men by the hand and led them to my secret spot, pointing to the ladder and waiting for liftoff.

In my twenties, dating in New York City was a lot like climbing that building in a blackout. I could never quite remember where I was going, who I was with, or how I had gotten there. I downloaded all the apps and got dressed up for first dates at wine bars, dive bars, and themed bars. I hoisted my hopes onto men I barely knew, convincing myself that everything was fine even when a voice in my head was whispering otherwise.

My drinking made it challenging to form genuine connections with the men I met. When I was twenty-four, I went on a marathon date with a Financial Analyst who was a self-described bookworm. We spent six hours drinking and talking, ordering round after round of cocktails as we inched our bar stools closer to each other. I was proud of my ability to go drink for drink with him; I felt empowered and flirty, liberated by our libations. *This is the best date ever,* the analyst kept repeating. Outside, he hailed me a cab just as it started to snow. Then, in one of those magic New York moments, he leaned in and kissed me.

The next morning, as I tried to give my roommate a play by play of our incredible connection, I realized I couldn't quite remember all the details. The following weekend, when we met up at a birthday party for one of his friends, everything felt awkward between us. I got too drunk, blacked out, and never heard from him again.

I always felt so empowered when I drank with the guys, but the truth is far less feminist: most of the times I drank, I did it for boys. For attention, for the male gaze, for affection, for love.

I drank because it turned me into the kind of girl guys wanted. This isn't a theory plucked out of my imagination. It was a method I tested carefully over the years with the precision of a scientist, removing variables like feelings and keeping control groups like myself. When I was sober, I flirted awkwardly, my limbs weighing me down. I was painfully aware of my skin, my hips, my boring everything. But with alcohol, I flitted gracefully from one topic to the next. I was a skilled conversationalist, confidently launching into conversational Italian I didn't know I remembered. I became a more charming version of myself: funnier, thinner, sugary sweet. And men responded. They flirted back, bought me drinks, took me home. I wanted the perfect love story with the perfect guy, and I needed alcohol to get it.

I was drunk the night of my first kiss in high school, and again when I had sex for the first time in college. Drinking was a magic elixir that brought me closer to the opposite sex. As I became well-versed in hookup culture, I came to regard alcohol as a kind of truth serum that revealed our real selves. I loved spending nights lying awake with boys I had just met, spilling the secrets we normally guarded fiercely, knowing all would be erased when the sun came up. There was a silent agreement: we could be vulnerable with each other under the influence, just as long as we both pretended not to remember the next day.

At twenty-five, I woke up in bed next to a friend of a friend. It was my first real one-night stand, and I laughed off the blurry details of the night before; we had both been sloppy. But over time, the same scene became less cute. At twenty-seven, I woke up next to a stranger. As my hangover wedged its way into my throat, panic came over me. We were naked, but I couldn't remember what had happened the night before. There were bits and pieces of memories: the bar we met at, our fourth round of drinks, kissing in a taxi. When he rolled over and I got a good look at his face, I almost started crying. I didn't even know if I liked him.

Still, I was in love with the idea of love and liquor. I didn't want to be the girl slurring over her wine, but I also didn't know how I would ever fall in love without it. Alcohol, according to my research, was the key to unlocking intimacy. All around me, friends were falling in love with men they met over drinks. But as my blackouts and hangovers became worse, it became clear that cocktails weren't bringing me any closer to love—they were holding me back.

Even though alcohol wasn't doing my love life any favors,

I worried about dating sober; nothing felt more daunting or intimidating. I was twenty-eight, and every date I had ever been on revolved around alcohol. In addition to feeling like a bumbling teenager, I had no idea how to maneuver the logistics around planning and communicating that, yes, I was interested in getting drinks but, no, I would not be drinking. The idea of re-entering the pool without my trusted life vest was alarming.

My first few months of sober dating were a mishmash. I experimented with different methods of disclosing my sobriety, from sending a heads-up text message to "casually" dropping it into conversation mid-date. I tested different explanations too. I'm on a cleanse, alcohol has been messing with my sleep, I'm taking a break, I'm on new medication. But the reactions—the new variable I couldn't control— were mixed.

My first sober date could barely conceal his shock when I ordered a seltzer. *I've been getting really bad hangovers,* I tried to explain in a rush. *I'm just taking a break.* But he wasn't satisfied. *Have you tried just drinking tequila?* His face was serious, like he had been tasked with solving a grave problem. *Tequila never gives me a hangover. Or maybe,* he sighed defeatedly, *just sangria?* When I tried to change the subject, he waved the waiter over to cancel our appetizer order.

Other dates tried to appear understanding. An investment banker had an uncle who was, he whispered with a grimace, *an alcoholic.* On a coffee date with a "serial entrepreneur," I shared that I hadn't had a drink in three months. *That's a great way to lose weight,* he nodded approvingly.

Then there was sex without alcohol. My first time was with Ian, a hookup buddy who lived in San Francisco. We slept together a couple of times a year, usually after a night of drinking, whenever he was back home in New York City for the holidays. I knew I could expect a text message from him when I started seeing Christmas lights going up in my neighborhood. The sex was always good, followed by thirty minutes of polite catch-up chit chat. We were friends, or something like it.

I stopped drinking in September, and Ian texted me like clockwork that Thanksgiving. Was I free to hang out sometime after midnight? It was a textbook booty call, but I didn't know when my next chance to have sex would be. I felt like I did in high school: desperate to lose my sober virginity. I told him to come over when he was free and made myself coffee so I could stay awake. I applied under-eye concealer and mascara. I lit a candle, then blew it out. I took selfies of my face and pretended not to watch the clock.

Ian's visit lasted less than an hour, and when I got back in bed after he left, I felt empty. I brought the blankets all the way up to my chin like I was sick. I couldn't put my finger on where I had encountered this hollowness before. Then, I remembered: I had felt it in the moments right after a drunken hookup ended and before I passed out. I saw flashes of myself at bars, desperate to feel close to another human. I realized I had been lying to myself when I said I didn't want something serious or with strings attached. I wanted the strings that came with sex; without them, sex just felt transactional. It was easier to ignore this feeling after drunken sex; I was too busy nursing a hangover to listen to my inner voice. But after Ian left that night, I felt an ache that reminded me of homesickness. It was as though I was missing something or someone I hadn't even met yet. So I decided I would try sleeping with people I had romantic feelings toward.

Finding someone I had an authentic connection with was my next challenge. Even in sobriety, I was as obsessed with alcohol as I had been when I was drinking. At ten months sober, I went on a few dates with a neighbor who worked in sales. He was mild-mannered, polite, and texted when he said he would. But the main reason I kept seeing him was that he didn't think it was weird that I didn't drink. In conversations with friends, I cited his nonchalance about my sobriety as if it were a personality trait. *Is he interesting? Funny?* a friend asked on a walk in the West Village as I filled her in on our latest date. I shrugged. It was only when I felt nothing after our third makeout that I realized my feelings were neutral at best. I called things off before they went further.

Having genuine feelings for someone, I discovered, also came with its own set of issues. When I met Mike, a curly haired engineer who lived in Brooklyn and loved hot yoga, I felt butterflies for the first time since college. Only now, I had no idea how I used to flirt when I liked a guy. I tried to channel my former lush self for a flicker of how she used to seduce men in bars. Where were the easy jokes and casual compliments I lobbed at men when I was drunk? Without alcohol I felt like I was thirteen again, covered in acne, and sporting uncomfortable braces and a training bra. I seriously considered buying books like *How to Flirt: A Practical Guide,* but worried about my imaginary boyfriend uncovering it someday. *Wait, you bought a book to learn how to flirt?* I pictured him turning the paperback over in disgust. *We are so over.* I embarked on a course in sober flirtation, enlisting friends for support.

R u sitting next to each other? my friend Arielle texted me during a date with Mike. Just try touching his knee mid convo. I extended my pointer finger and brought it dangerously close to his kneecap before chickening out. Later, Arielle demonstrated that she had been referring to more of a caress than a pointed tap. There was so much to learn.

With Mike, I experimented with the art of withholding. I went to a party on his rooftop and filled a plastic cup with water, pretending it was a mixed drink. When we met up late on a Friday night, he was already buzzed and assumed I was too; I didn't correct him. The morning after we slept together for the first time, he rolled in my direction with a groan. *Man, I'm hungover,* he murmured into my hair. I said nothing. On another date, over grilled octopus, I ordered a Diet Coke. It was a sticky summer night in Brooklyn and Mike nodded appreciatively. *A cold soda sounds good. I'll get one too.* He had no idea I wasn't getting a soda to be nostalgic or cute. As I started getting more excited about him, hiding my sobriety started to feel wrong. When I finally confessed that I didn't drink at all, I could tell Mike was bewildered, replaying all those nights he thought we had both been tipsy. When he ended things shortly afterward, he swore it wasn't me; he just wasn't ready for a relationship. But I was crushed by his rejection and couldn't help but wonder if he had been spooked by my secret sobriety. A few weeks later, I saw him walking around Brooklyn holding hands with another girl.

With time, as my insecurities about being sober faded, I started to feel more empowered on dates. I realized how much of my agency I was giving to total strangers and started to appreciate my new sober powers. I had always approached dating with a "pick me" mentality: I wanted to make the cut for date number two. And when I was drinking, I liked pretty much everyone. But without the haze of alcohol, I became a more discerning judge of character. I started paying attention to how I felt on dates and asking myself if I even liked the person on the other side of the table. After three perfectly fine dates with a cute guy who lived in my building, I admitted I didn't feel a spark. Instead of letting his texts go unanswered, I told him the truth, something I had learned how to do in sobriety. When we bumped into each other in the elevator a few weeks later it was slightly awkward, but not because I had blacked out or ghosted him. I was starting to like who I was becoming without alcohol: I felt happier and more comfortable with myself.

Sex also became more intentional and less transactional. Instead of only meeting up with someone after a night of drinking and seeing sex as a sign that he liked me, I began to see it as an egalitarian act. Sober sex was still occasionally awkward, as sex can be when tequila isn't smoothing out the edges, but it could also be great. And for the first time, it was about my own pleasure. I discovered what I liked, and it was empowering.

After all the beer bongs and late-night smoking sessions, being sober and having control over my body and mind was my most feminist act yet. Because I was starting to like who I was becoming, I became a stronger advocate for myself and what I was looking for in a partner. I grew more discerning of my dates' character traits and started to pay attention to my inner voice. And when I felt a real connection with someone, I paid attention.

I had been sober for a little over a year when I met Adam. He didn't fit my checklist: he lived in Los Angeles, was very opinionated, and was shorter than the desired height range I had selected on my dating apps. (For the record, my range was absurd and arbitrary. I'm 5'4", yet for some reason I set my desired height minimum at 5'11". Adam is 5'9" and wouldn't have even shown up as a potential match on an app.) Despite my hesitation, a mutual friend had introduced us, so I gave him a chance. On our first date in Brooklyn, he ordered a cocktail and I tossed back a cappuccino, hoping the caffeine would keep me energized. Adam let me take the lead when it came to discussing my sobriety. He had a few questions (Was it okay if he ordered a drink? Yes.) but his inquiries were warm and considerate. Drinks turned into dinner, and as I examined his face in the candlelight, I was surprised to feel an undercurrent of electricity buzzing beneath my skin. I liked him.

In our early dates, I learned that even good feelings can be unbearable in the way that they snake themselves around you. Adam quickly went from a stranger to someone I could really care about, and that was terrifying. Because we spent weeks at a time apart in between his work trips to New York, we talked on the phone most nights, a habit I hadn't indulged in since high school. It was a little awkward, but it was also sweet. When we spoke, we took turns asking each other questions from the popular *New York Times* essay on the thirty-six questions that lead to love. We raced through the easy ones (What would constitute a "perfect" day for you? For what in your life do you feel most grateful?) and grew closer as our questions and answers became more vulnerable. When I asked Adam question #18 about his most terrible memory, he told me about the summer four friends had drowned on their day off at the camp where they all worked. Question #24, how do you feel about your mother, was when I told Adam about the year my mom had spent in treatment for breast cancer and described how I drank heavily to quiet my fears. When I was drinking, I spilled (or slurred) all my secrets at once to anyone who would listen. Now, I had the patience and confidence to take my time sharing with a partner who truly cared.

This isn't to say I wasn't occasionally freaked by how well everything was going. When Adam invited me to meet him for a weekend in San Francisco, I panicked at the thought of sharing a hotel room with him. It was so intimate. What if I had bad morning breath or woke up with a pimple that he saw before I had time to hide it? I bought new pajamas and packed four more sweaters than I needed. Because I was missing my normal weekend recovery meeting, I decided to squeeze one in while we were there. I had gone from a girl who was terrified to tell strangers she didn't drink to a young woman who was confident enough to tell her new boyfriend that she needed an hour to herself for a twelve-step recovery meeting. I asked a friend from the Bay Area for recommendations, and she sent me a meeting near our hotel. To his credit, Adam made it easy for me to be the confident, authentic version of myself I was becoming. When the meeting was over, I walked outside to find him waiting for me with an iced coffee, a donut, and a flower.

Falling in love in sobriety was exhilarating and uncomfortable all at once. Now I had something new to lose, to miss, to ruin. And that was an excellent reason to drink. Adam sent me sweet, thoughtful gifts, like gummy bears when I published a new article or Band-Aids and socks when I complained about the blisters forming from my new sneakers. I found myself wondering if I deserved something this good and feeling my way around the edges of our new relationship for a self-destruct button. I wanted to be with him, but I also wanted to ruin things before they could ruin me.

Despite my fears and attempts at self-sabotage, I knew my connection with Adam was different from any crush or relationship I had been in before. Unlike previous relationships, there were no drunken fights or accusations about who he was texting when we weren't together. We cared about each other; I helped him get back into exercise after a knee injury, and he remembered which recovery meetings were my favorites and made plans around them. Even though we had arguments, I was always grateful the morning after when I woke up and remembered it all; no memory was cringeworthy or slightly out of focus. I saw Adam clearly, and he saw me.

Over the next two years, we traveled to five countries, met each other's families, and moved in together. When COVID-19 hit and New York went into lockdown, our honeymoon phase came to a screeching halt. In quarantine, we heard sirens blaring past our Brooklyn window all night and watched the death tolls rise on the news every morning. Adam grew a beard, and I spent every day in sweatpants. Like the rest of the world, we were scared. Stressed and anxious, Adam started drinking at night in our apartment. He had never drunk alone at home before, but I understood: the bars and restaurants where he typically drank with friends were all shuttered. Still, it was challenging to see his empty beer cans in the trash night after night. Was I not enough? Why did he need to drink when we were alone together? I logged onto my virtual recovery meetings daily and reminded myself that he had his own relationship with alcohol. Before quarantine, we were both busy and having dinner together was a treat. Now, we sat at the same table night after night with nothing new to talk about. Some nights, as he snored next to me, I missed the part of our relationship where we missed each other.

We were different versions of ourselves on the other side of quarantine, but we made it through together, sweatpants and all. We had to have difficult conversations as businesses reopened and we discovered we had different comfort levels when it came to new variables like outdoor dining and seeing unmasked friends. I could never have shown up for these challenging discussions when I was still drinking; we talked about our futures, our financial insecurities, and our implicit biases. These were tougher questions to answer than the ones posed as we fell in love, but they still brought us closer together.

When our lease was up, we left New York for Los Angeles. The warm weather was healing for both of us: we started doing California activities like going on long hikes and buying local produce from the farmers' market. And then, after one Wednesday morning hike, Adam asked me to marry him.

I spent my teens and twenties drinking to attract a man. But my drinking was blocking me from the kind of love I desperately wanted. The night Adam proposed, we celebrated over good food and drinks. Adam ordered his favorite cocktail, a Negroni, and I had sparkling water. As I looked up at the moonlight and down at my ring, there was no part of me that wished I was drunk. I had always worried it would feel sad to forgo a champagne toast when I got engaged, but I was anything but sad. Sobriety had given me the kind of love I had been searching for in every bar. Most importantly, it had allowed me to become the kind of woman who could show up for a relationship.

When I allowed myself to be vulnerable and real in sobriety, I was able to attract the partner of my dreams. It isn't always perfect, but it's real. And that, reader, beats any buzz.

PART III

SOBER

9

Alcoholism Needs a Makeover

I need to clear something up. I didn't stop partying because I was trying to achieve some state of enlightenment or hop on a wellness trend. I loved drinking too much for that. I got sober because alcohol was destroying my life. And I didn't do it alone.

I first learned about alcoholism when I was eleven. I eavesdropped on my mom's phone calls to piece the story together: my aunt was an alcoholic, which meant she did things like get drunk in the afternoon before driving to pick up my nine-year-old cousin from a playdate. On their way home one day, my aunt lost control of her car, flipping it over twice in the process. When my mom spoke to my uncle after the accident she whispered, *I'm so sorry,* like someone had died even though my aunt and cousin had both survived with injuries. My aunt had been court or-dered to attend rehab.

When I blacked out, I did it like other twenty-somethings: before crawling into an Uber or a stranger's bed. But I thought about my aunt from time to time as my hangovers started to get worse. With my head dangling into the toilet, I wondered what her drinking had looked like when she was my age, and if it had started out feeling like magic be-fore morphing into something darker.

I didn't know anyone my age who was sober, so I thought I was doomed to repeat the same cycle (drink, puke, repent) until an external force snapped me out of it. A new job, maybe, or a hypothetical husband and baby. It seemed impossible that I would be able to take care of a baby with alcohol poisoning and a splitting headache. I imagined that, by then, my drinking would just work itself out.

By the time my twenty-eighth birthday rolled around, I was confronted by a few uncomfortable truths: I blacked out nearly every time I drank. I routinely had to skip out on plans after a night of drinking because of my horrible hangovers. I rarely went out on more than two or three dates with the same person, and I struggled to form mean-ingful connections. My friendships were subsisting on vodka sodas and rosé, and I gossiped about everyone, even the people I cared about.

I had tried to moderate my drinking before. Only one glass of wine at dinner, no more than four cocktails at the bar, no tequila shots, etc. But these guidelines never worked.

To me, one glass of wine is a waste of calories. I truly don't understand the point. I drink to get drunk; there is no in between. And it's not like people were forcing me to take shots. After a drink or two, I was the one corralling the group to the bar and assembling lime wedges. It became a compulsion: once alcohol touched my lips, I was a different person. Still, I had a job and didn't drink alone in my apartment or first thing in the morning. I clung to these truths because they meant I couldn't have a "real" drinking problem.

But the morning after I woke up in bed next to my boss's friend with no memory of how I had gotten there, I realized it didn't matter if my drinking problem qualified as "real." I needed to stop, and it was clear, through years of trial and error, that I couldn't do it myself. So, I did what once seemed impossible: I walked into a twelve-step recovery meeting.

Because of television and movies, I thought twelve-step meetings looked like a group of older men sitting in a circle in a dingy church basement. These men were nothing like me, therefore I couldn't possibly need help from people like them. They drank straight from the bottle every morning, I imagined, divorced their wives, and had ruddy cheeks.

In addition to my own outdated stereotypes about people with alcohol use disorder, there were also a handful of terrifying articles about recovery I had stumbled upon in the past. Years earlier, after a bad night out in the East Village, I lay in my bed ransacking the Internet for clues on how to manage my drinking. I found an article that tore apart the framework for twelve-step programs, citing their lack of modern science and one-size-fits-all approach as major downfalls. Another story published in a national newspaper made similar points. A female blogger published several posts about why meetings hadn't worked for her. Desperate for an alternative, I wrote to her, asking for advice. Was there something else that might help me stop drinking? But she never wrote back.

Twelve-step programs are not the only way to get sober, and they might not be for everyone. But the information I found online left me feeling more isolated than before. I came to believe this recovery model was outdated, archaic, and designed by and for men. There was also a noticeable lack of firsthand accounts and information available online, likely because most recovery programs are anonymous. I remember feeling crushed: years of therapy hadn't helped my drinking, moderation wasn't working, and now it appeared that young women who drink until they blackout— AKA, me—might not be represented in recovery programs. I didn't know what to do.

Years later, I was finally desperate enough to stop blacking out and living my life on a hungover hamster wheel. And that desperation is what got me in the door of my first meeting, in all its controversial glory. Despite the mixed reviews, I had simply run out of alternative options.

On my way to that first meeting, I stuffed my hands in my pockets and prepared to avoid eye contact with anyone I encountered. Like any good Millennial, I had turned to Google for guidance and discovered a women's group that met in my neighborhood after work. I expected to walk into a room of women with whom I would have nothing in common. My expectations for the night were incredibly low. For the first time in my life, I didn't care about socializing or finding the "right" group of friends. These women could have been my opposites in every way, but if they had the secret to a life without blackouts, I wanted to hear it.

I rolled my eyes as I walked up to the address on my phone: a church. What a cliché. A sign with an arrow pointed me down a flight of stairs and I flinched, wishing I were invisible. I braced myself for whatever awkward scene I was about to encounter downstairs. I came to a full stop as I rounded the corner and entered the meeting space. Unlike what I had seen in movies, this room was bright, warm, and filled with women in their twenties and thirties laughing and talking together. I couldn't believe how *normal* they all looked, and I wondered if they were all taking the same multivitamin because their complexions looked amazing. They seemed healthy, confident, and strangely happy. I thought all eyes would be on me as I slid into my seat, clearly new, but the group remained immersed in their own conversations until a woman moved to the front of the room and announced that the meeting was about to start.

I don't remember much from that first meeting, but I do remember this: I related to the stories I heard. These women drank like I drank. They blacked out and felt the same overwhelming shame and isolation I experienced after a spree.

But now that they were sober, they also seemed to be okay. Like, more than okay. They had important jobs and engagement rings and shared stories about best friends and meaningful relationships with their families. These details might sound trivial in retrospect, but I was terrified about never finding love or purpose in a life without alcohol. Hearing about a promotion at work and seeing a baby bump in a recovery meeting were the superficial beacons of hope that I desperately needed. It all seemed so impossible to me; when a pregnant woman in her thirties shared that she was celebrating ten years sober, I genuinely thought she must have been lying.

My head was spinning when I re-emerged unscathed an hour later. Nothing groundbreaking had happened; I hadn't raised my hand to share, and no one had forced me to disclose my name or Social Security number. And yet, as I walked home, I felt different. Where there was once fear and dread, I now felt a tiny flicker of optimism. Maybe I could do this.

I went back the next week and the one after that. I attended different groups, too, observing their customs like an anthropologist. And something magical happened: I heard my stories in theirs. I stuck to the women's groups and began to discover a new kind of life. These women were sophisticated, intelligent, and sober. They all seemed to possess the kind of inner peace and happiness I had been looking for in every drink, workout class, and first date. And they also seemed to genuinely enjoy attending meetings.

Over time, I began to understand why. I started to feel safe in these cozy rooms and was continuously surprised by how welcoming they felt. Women took turns bringing snacks, and a table in the back was often filled with candy, popcorn, and cookies. There was a powerful sense of community, and I found myself feeling calmer after each meeting I attended.

Still, I struggled with the labels—being sober carried such a negative stigma and I was ashamed of what it said about me. Sobriety meant admitting I was powerless over alcohol; that it had made my life unmanageable. I couldn't handle how pathetic that sounded. I had a job, friends, and an apartment; how unmanageable was that? I was a high-achieving, well-educated woman who had been raised to believe I could tackle any obstacle if I worked hard enough. Admitting powerlessness felt like failure.

But the truth was, I was powerless over alcohol. When I drank, I lost control. In the presence of alcohol, I put myself in dangerous situations, woke up next to strangers, and lost huge chunks of my memory. When I put it on paper, it didn't sound all that manageable. I started to realize I was applying outdated logic to the way I drank. I had no problem admitting I struggled with anxiety or depression; these terms had been destigmatized in mainstream culture. Talking about mental health issues was almost trendy. So why did the word *alcoholism*—also referred to as *alcohol use disorder*—sound so disgraceful? I had been carrying around shame over my body's response to alcohol, but what was wrong with being powerless over a powerful substance? A person with a peanut allergy is powerless over peanuts, and she doesn't keep trying to eat peanut butter to reclaim her power. A few months into sobriety, it hit me: the insanity of my drinking was my inability to accept that it wasn't serving me. Once I fully accepted that I simply couldn't drink safely, I felt an incredible amount of relief. I didn't have to work harder to be "better" at drinking. I could just not drink.

Despite my initial reticence, meetings were also helping me stay sober. The stories I heard from other young people in recovery made me feel a lot less alone and helped me understand my own drinking. I would wake up in the morning feeling cranky and anxious and leave a meeting a few hours later feeling infinitely better. I couldn't explain it, but it was enough to keep me going back. Maybe, if meetings were the "medicine," I had the thing they had been designed to treat.

About two months after my first meeting, I shared about how nervous I was for my first sober wedding that upcoming weekend. Other girls in the room nodded knowingly as I listed my fears; how would I make it through cocktail hour and dancing without a drink? What would I say if someone offered me a glass of bubbly? A blonde who appeared to be around my age approached me after the meeting and asked for my phone number. She had gone to her first sober wedding that summer and promised to call me the next day. Her name was Alex. It was November and she was rocking a head-to-toe winter-white ensemble, which I thought was just about the chicest thing I had ever seen. (If anyone knows how to wear all white without spilling on it, please let me know.)

The next day, Alex called me on her lunch break. I left my office to answer the call and walked in nervous circles around my building as we spoke. I worried she might grill me about my drinking or ask me personal questions I didn't want to answer. Instead, she launched into an easy conversation like we had been friends for years. *I know a sober wedding sounds so scary, but you're going to be fine,* she started before pausing to order herself a salad from Chop't. I heard the background sounds of Midtown Manhattan through the phone and relaxed into the familiar cacophony. I was comforted by the sounds of her busy, big life. *Okay, I'm back. Just remember, you don't have to stay the whole time. No one is paying attention to what's in your glass; just keep a full seltzer with lime on you the whole time. And if you start to feel tired, chug a Diet Coke or coffee.*

When I got back to my desk, I felt strangely calm. On Saturday night, sometime between the ceremony and cocktail hour, Alex texted me to check in on how I was feeling. I couldn't believe that she had remembered. It dawned on me that twelve-step programs had an added benefit. They meant that I didn't have to navigate the foreign waters of sobriety alone. I stuck around those groups and leaned into a secret sober sisterhood I had never known existed. Slinking into a meeting with a hot coffee and listening to people tell their stories became my version of church. Over the next two years, I would attend groups in France, Australia, Maine, Oregon, and California, and connect with people I would have never met otherwise. The longer I stuck around, the more interesting my life got.

Despite my growing comfort in meetings, I still carried shame about the label. Sobriety was my dirty little secret for most of the first year. I didn't tell my parents or friends I was attending recovery meetings, making up excuses about going to work events every night of the week. I told my college friends I was taking a break from drinking because it was making me anxious, but that didn't explain my vanishing act. Finally, my friend Arielle asked me out to dinner.

When we met at a Japanese restaurant in Williamsburg, she had questions. *Are you just sitting on your couch alone every night?* she asked point blank between bites of sushi. *It's great that you're not drinking anymore, but aren't you lonely?*

I hadn't known when, exactly, I would tell my friends the truth about going to meetings, and it seemed like Arielle had made the decision for me.

I'm not sitting on my couch every night, I started, swirling wasabi and soy sauce together with a chopstick. *I've, um, been going to these meetings. They kind of help. They're not as weird as I thought they would be and lots of young people go. It was my therapist's idea.* The words came out in a rush. Even just hearing myself say them out loud made me feel dramatic, and I instantly regretted telling her the truth. Tacking on a mention of my therapist (who was supportive of meetings but not the one to suggest them) seemed to add a bit of credibility to the whole thing while shirking some responsibility. It's not like it was my idea or anything.

Arielle paused as she digested the information, and my

stomach flopped. We had been friends for ten years, but
Arielle could be tough. She was bright, the most direct of
all our friends, and could be a little bit scary. *That's great*,
she announced decisively as she picked up another piece of
salmon. Then she made what is still one of the most insight-
ful comments I have heard about sobriety, both in and out
of recovery rooms. *You know how people used to think sexual
assault was just something that happened between two strangers
in an alley but now we're learning that it's more nuanced? Maybe
drinking is like that. Maybe what we think a drinking problem is
versus what it really looks like is changing.*

Her words were so simple, but they made so much sense.
Having a drinking problem had an outdated stigma, and
maybe the shame associated with it was outdated too. I instantly felt more comfortable, and with Arielle's support I
shared the truth with other close friends about where I had
been spending so much of my time. When I reached one year
sober, Arielle and a few of my best girlfriends from college
came to a women's meeting to see me celebrate. Afterward,
we went to a greasy diner down the block for French fries
and milkshakes.

A couple of years after I got sober, an essay was published in a major publication about why twelve-step programs were harmful to women. The piece described how
the program was created in the 1930s by a group of white
men who knew nothing about feminism. Today's woman,
the piece concluded, didn't need to renounce her power to
beat drinking.

I thought about the article for weeks. Had I read it when

I was twenty-four, it would have been the perfect excuse to continue my precarious cycle of blacking out and avoid seeking help. In writing about sobriety, the author of this piece had helped shed some of the stigma around it. But portraying twelve-step programs as archaic and patriar-chal struck me as dangerous. I wondered how many other young women had curiously read the story before clicking out of their browsers, resigning themselves to another year of blackouts and hangovers. I hated to think of the drink-ers who now thought they didn't "qualify" for recovery or envisioned it as a group of crusty old men waiting to rob women of their power. It took me another few years to accept that, although sobriety had been life changing for me, I could not control the way everyone else perceived recovery.

Long after my resistance to labels had been addressed, I continued to cringe at one key phrase in recovery: rock bottom. Much like my early impressions of sobriety, I asso-ciated rock bottom with an entangled mess of stereotypes and rules. I thought hitting rock bottom meant things like drinking on the job, getting fired, being institutionalized, losing one's home or family, and living on the street. I told myself my drinking had all been so ordinary. I was em-ployed, exercised regularly, and had never been on the re-ceiving end of an intervention. In fact, many of my friends and family members had questions about my decision to get sober. (*Are you sure? Not even a glass of wine? Why is it so hard for you to stop after one?*)

It took me years to understand that the outsides didn't

matter; the shame, anxiety, frustration, and loneliness I felt after I drank qualified me for sobriety. And in time, I learned that rock bottom, like anything else, looks different for different people. Just like my perfect day (a long walk, coffee, a cheese plate, and a good book) might sound average to someone else, my rock bottom didn't have to match a universal rubric. It was just the moment I stopped digging. There was freedom in unraveling this matted concept and finding space for my own experience in between the twisted knots.

Ironically, the more sobriety stories I heard, the lower my rock bottom became. I discovered my former default settings (uneasy, jealous, impulsive) were not the norm. I also learned that not everyone blacked out, even people who drank every day. I watched eyes widen as I shared stories about the hours I lost in blackouts; big, burly men in meetings seemed horrified by my tales of waking up in strangers' apartments and hospital rooms. I began to understand that, despite how normalized my work-hard, play-hard lifestyle had been, my rock bottom wasn't as cute as I initially believed.

I still think about my friend Arielle's comments often. I hope that the social stigma around alcohol use disorder, treatment modalities, and sobriety shifts one day. But until then, I'm trying to keep it simple. I think about my recovery meetings in the same way I think about yoga classes: they are a practice and part of my routine that allow me to show up as a present participant in my life. Along the way, they taught me to ask for help, introduced me to women who built big lives without a drink, and offered me a place to go when I felt lost. Most of all, they gave me what I searched for in every cocktail: the deepest, purest, and most genuine belief that everything was going to be okay. For that, and so much more, I'm grateful.

10

Dressing the Part

I had hoped getting sober would bring stability to all areas of my life. Every time I turned down a cocktail, *one day at a time,* I pictured it paying off. The serenity, the reserve of self-esteem, the clear skin. In all my fantasies, I also envisioned myself solving a problem that had plagued me since elementary school: getting dressed.

Dressing myself was always a chore. I had little interest in my clothes, with one exception. I was born to a French dad and American mom and grew up visiting my family in France every summer. On these trips, my grandmother took me shopping. She picked out my clothes for school: plaid skirts, collared shirts, thick tights, scarves, and coats. On my birthday, I always received a package from my grandparents containing neatly pressed pajama sets, sweaters, or a dress. At the French American School in New York, I always felt different around the other kids. Not quite French enough, but not fully American either. But when I showed up at school in the outfits my grandmother picked out for me, I felt secure and happy.

In fourth grade, my parents moved us to the suburbs of New Jersey. At my new school, no one wore plaid skirts or collared shirts. The girls wore flared jeans, butterfly clips, and twin sets. Suddenly, my French clothes felt embarrassing and childish. On my second day of school, I met a curly haired girl named Maya who informed me that she was going to be a fashion designer when she grew up and asked me if I wanted to be best friends. On playdates at Maya's house, she showed me her sketchbook and I flipped through it in awe. I had no idea there was so much to know about clothes. Drawings of girls wearing bell bottom jeans and Limited Too–inspired tops filled the pages. Her confidence was impressive: at nine, she knew what styles she liked, how to put an outfit together, and where to shop. All my old clothes were wrong; I needed to look like the other girls.

When I came home from Maya's one morning after a sleepover, I called my parents into the kitchen. *Look,* I exclaimed proudly, pulling a sheet of paper out of my backpack. I had drawn my own figurines, carefully copying Maya's lines and outfitting the girls in jeans and floral skirts. My dad raised his eyebrows. *Well,* he managed to get out. *I don't think there should be any more sleepovers at Maya's.*

He hated when I tried to be like the other girls, implored me to stay true to my own interests and hobbies. It was true that sketching clothes had been Maya's idea, but my dad's reaction left me feeling silly. I absorbed the implication that thinking about clothes was frivolous, which became a source of confusion. As women, we receive messaging around the importance of our appearances from the time we are small. I struggled with these two contradictory ideas: that fashion was foolish, but that how I put myself together was also a representation of my worth.

As my body changed over the years, shopping became more of an ordeal. I sobbed in fitting rooms as my mom waited outside, begging me to come out and just show her the jeans. I hated my hips, my breasts, my stomach. In college, when I learned to restrict my food intake and started exercising, shopping became slightly more endurable. I was introduced to clothing that was meant to signal to the opposite sex, and I purchased carbon copies of the miniskirts and heels I saw other girls wearing at bars.

My uniform for class was a North Face fleece and yoga pants or a pair of jeans and crew neck sweater. I oscillated between exhibiting and concealing my body, ruled by insecurities in both scenarios. I wasn't vying for best dressed; I just wanted to slide by undetected and pass as put together.

When I got ready for a party, a drink always made it that much easier to get dressed. I would put on a playlist with my roommates, pour myself a vodka and orange juice, and put on my go-to skinny black jeans and halter top. There were other nights where I longed to feel special, a rumbling in my stomach threatening to erupt in a scream. I couldn't stand to face my own closet. My stylish girlfriends were generous, lending me dresses that made me feel like a new person. I wondered how they always seemed to have the perfect outfit teed up and why they never seemed to be scrambling at the last minute like me.

(Cut to me the day before a big party, buying a pair of shoes that are on sale but are also half a size too small and will pinch my toes until I bleed. Me at the Halloween store an hour before it closes, riffling through masks and discarded cat ears.)

I didn't care about myself enough to shop in advance or dress my body as if I liked it. I had no problem spending my money on alcohol, but clothes and shoes were a different story. I didn't feel deserving of beautiful possessions. Instead, I ordered items on final sale, squeezing myself into them when they didn't fit right and going through my roommates' closets. My college boyfriend always got angry with me whenever I borrowed outfits from friends. *It's weird when you wear their clothes. It feels like you're trying to be someone else.* I didn't know how to tell him that was the point.

Learning to shop and get dressed was one of those life skills I told myself I would naturally get around to mastering someday. In my twenties, I would wake up the morning after a blackout and stuff my bloated body into leggings and a sweatshirt. *One day,* I would think as I watched well-dressed girls strutting down New York sidewalks. I wondered what magazines or blogs they were all reading, how they learned about trends, where they found the confidence to develop a sense of personal style. I only shopped at the last minute and bought trendy fast fashion items regardless of whether I liked them. I was ashamed of my big breasts, so I only ordered oversized shirts or sweaters. I hated my wide hips, so I didn't let myself order fitted dresses or two-piece bathing suits. I saw clothes as a mechanism for hiding.

In my first year sober, as my brain fog cleared, I decided it was time to learn how to get dressed. I followed fashion bloggers on social media and ordered the jeans and sweaters they linked. I had no idea what I felt good in, so I bought random items: overalls, bright sweaters, lipstick, rompers, velvet bodysuits. I stopped into boutiques I had never visited on my way home from work and tried on new styles. *Maybe it's time to stop wearing sacks,* my friend Nina suggested helpfully when I showed up to dinner wearing a baggy dress. I made a note to myself: no more sacks.

But I underestimated how much I still craved quiet chaos. At two years sober, when I found myself sweating in a dressing room on the day before a friend's wedding, I realized I needed more help. I had known about this weekend for over six months, yet I had not planned my outfits. I went to seven boutiques that afternoon, hating how I looked in every dress they had, cursing myself the whole time. I finally found a light green dress an hour before the rehearsal dinner and made it to the event just as it was starting. I didn't know what was wrong with me. Did I crave the high and rush that came from my chaotic, last-minute shopping escapades? Why didn't I want better for myself?

It had taken real work and time to maintain my sobriety.

It turned out that rebuilding my relationship with clothes would not be all that different.

* * *

SOMETIME AFTER I stopped erasing my memories with alcohol, my grandmother started losing her own.

Lewy body dementia, we learned, is a progressive type of dementia that causes vivid hallucinations and a decline in thinking, reasoning, and independent function. My grandmother had always been beautiful, whip smart, and elegant. She was Jackie O meets Marie Curie, a pharmacist who smelled like Chanel perfume. She wore a skirt and stockings with modest pumps every single day, even if she was just doing housework and running errands. When I hugged her and felt her soft cheek against my own, I could feel the love and attention she put into taking care of herself. *The progression of dementia with Lewy bodies is relentless,* Google warned.

Even when my grandmother started slipping away, she clung to her clothes. She dressed herself in the same lovely blouses and knit cardigans I knew by heart. She followed her skincare regimen daily, even when she started losing her keys in the medicine cabinets. When I visited her in France in my first year of sobriety, she offered me wine at dinner. *Sarah doesn't drink,* my grandfather corrected her quickly, shooting me an apologetic look. My grandmother looked confused and lowered her head to fidget with the zipper on her sweater. I reached out and squeezed her hand.

As we walked out of the restaurant after dinner, we brushed past a group of French women. I paused to take them in, all cigarette smoke, jeans, and button-down shirts. Their outfits were simple, but they carried themselves with an understated sophistication I recognized from my grand-mother. I felt a twinge of something familiar, a flopping sensation I had never been able to name before. Now, with a sober clarity, I could hear the voice in my head: *You don't look French enough, but you're not all American either.* If clothes told a story, what were mine saying?

I spent a summer studying abroad in Bologna, Italy, when I was twenty. One afternoon, just after lunch, I was sitting at a table outside a café, waiting for the check. I was alone, staring up at the sun, when an older man wearing a hat approached me. *Excusez-moi,* he began in French, *où est la basilique de San Petronio?* I was still learning my way around Bologna, but I knew the answer to this one. I gave him directions in French, and he thanked me be-fore turning in the opposite direction. *Monsieur,* I stopped him, a question I couldn't hold in. *Comment avez-vous su que j'étais française?* How did you know I was French? He smiled, his eyes twinkling. *Juste comme ça. C'est un regard.* It's a look.

I looked down at the tank top and denim shorts I had thrown on that morning; my outfit was nondescript, simple. But he had seen a spark of my identity anyway. I held his words close, a surprise gift that warmed me. I was bilin-gual and a French-American citizen, but I had always been self-conscious about the slight accent that crept in when I spoke French, or the way people cocked their heads at me when they heard my dad's name, *Jean-Marc.*

I adored my family in France and America; both felt like home. But I could never quite figure out how to present myself in either place. In Bologna, a stranger in a piazza had spotted something in me that I couldn't see in myself. Now, as I remembered his words years later, I realized I had to figure out how to believe him.

* * *

BACK IN NEW York, I called my friends and asked for help. *Can we go shopping together?* I felt like I was asking them to the prom. I was afraid to admit that I had no idea what I was doing when it came to choosing clothes and worried my friends would shake their heads, refusing to share their secrets. Instead, they were happy to help. They listed brand names like best friends and pulled blazers and dresses off hangers for me to try on. I trusted them: they were always showing up to brunches and dinners looking casually chic, wearing soft sweaters and great jeans. They made suggestions, but they also encouraged me to trust myself. It didn't matter if they liked it, they reminded me. I needed to feel good in it.

Bit by bit, I started to make progress. Every time I purchased an article of clothing I genuinely loved, it felt like a huge accomplishment. When I felt anxious in a store, I closed my eyes and reminded myself I deserved to feel good. And I employed the same cheesy slogans I had used when I first quit drinking. *One day at a time, easy does it, progress not perfection.*

I still had questions: where were people buying formal dresses that didn't make them hate themselves? When did I miss the memo on all the matching pajama sets? And how was everyone paying their rent and buying purses?

Bringing these queries to friends felt vulnerable, like I was missing some crucial chunk of girl gene. But their responses were constructive: they shared resources, weighed in on important shoe debates, and taught me about the best silhouettes for my body type, a phrase I had always rolled my eyes at. My friend Kat even started sending me links to dresses she thought would look good on me.

Without alcohol, I felt like I was meeting myself for the first time. The way I dressed and presented myself shifted as I learned more about who I was and what I liked. As I started paying more attention, I began to develop preferences. I liked jackets and blazers, started collecting vintage sweatshirts, and felt the most comfortable in jeans and a good white T-shirt. And because I was sober now, I trusted myself not to spill, drip, or throw up on my new clothes. Learning to get dressed wasn't about hiding or changing myself; it was an act of self-love, an amends for all the years of neglect.

One afternoon, I went through my closet and stacked all my old clothes into different piles. Keep, donate, sell. I sat on the floor for hours, my back aching as I moved through old shirts, dresses, jackets, and shoes. When I finally stood up, the sun was setting outside. I rolled a suitcase filled with my belongings to the Salvation Army, watching as a girl with a nose ring sorted through my old items. As I walked home, my empty luggage bouncing along the sidewalk behind me, I felt lighter too.

* * *

GETTING DRESSED WAS never about the clothes themselves; it was about how I felt in them.

I learned from an early age that being a woman meant being put together in so many ways: the way I spoke, how I kept my hair and fingernails, my academic and professional aspirations. In college, when I told a relative that my favorite course was about the criminal justice system, he wrinkled his nose. *That can be a very ugly world,* he said. *You might find that you enjoy some Art History classes instead.*

I was starving for outside approval in all areas and drinking and getting dressed were no exception. I wanted to wear the cool labels in middle school and drink the right way in high school. I paid attention to my peers and shapeshifted so I would fit in. I sought out short-term gratification in miniskirts and tequila shots and hoped they would make me feel desirable, but the next morning I still felt like an imposter. Like my drinking, I struggled with moderation when it came to my clothes; nothing was ever enough. I was either wearing the same skinny jeans every weekend or drunkenly online shopping every night. When I was spit out into the "real world" at twenty-two, I felt vulnerable and lost, so I kept hiding in my clothes and cups.

Clothes are just one way society teaches us to present ourselves, and our choices signal how we want to be perceived to the outside world. When I was drinking, my uniforms were manufactured and controlled, but they often became sloppy and chaotic. I ripped my tights when I fell on sidewalks, stained my tank tops with beer, and broke my heels in blackouts. Many people can drink and still present themselves in positive ways. But my relationship with alcohol was tampering with my sense of self, and my clothing reflected that.

According to a study conducted at Northwestern University, dressing in a certain way can influence your behavior and affect the way you perform at work and in life. Wearing a white coat that you believe belongs to a doctor, for instance, can make you more focused. Sobriety gave me permission to try on different white coats until I connected with the woman I wanted to become—someone creative, self-assured, and capable. Of course, it was always an inside job. Clothes didn't have the power to alter my emotional state, but they allowed me to deepen my burgeoning understanding of myself.

My clean clothes and streamlined wardrobe helped me signal that I was more confident in my identity when I stopped drinking. But getting dressed was just one way I learned to care for myself in sobriety. My mornings were another, a quiet stretch of time with coffee and my journal before starting the workday. Daily walks with no destination were also a favorite, just me and a good podcast or playlist. For other people, self-care might look like cooking more meals at home, joining a softball team, or painting. It doesn't matter, really. It all comes back to the same place: recognizing that, now, you have a choice in how you spend your time and present yourself. Without alcohol, I had the space to figure out who I was and how I wanted to walk through my life. The chic boots I wore along the way were just a bonus.

* * *

My grandmother's dementia lived up to its ruthless warning. She forgot our names and her stories and slurred when she spoke, her tongue struggling to form familiar words. Drinking had always been my favorite way to manage intense emotions, and the ones that sprouted up as my grandmother got sicker were excruciating. Her dementia reminded me of my blackouts, but her condition was not self-imposed, nor was it temporary. When I thought about the fact that she would never remember again, I wanted to scream or drink until I couldn't think. But it's hard to drink with a head full of sobriety; I knew getting drunk would only make my anxiety worse. So, I put on my big girl pants (jeans) and settled in for life on life's terms.

Within two years, my grandmother was living in the memory care unit of an assisted living home. Her floor required a special elevator code so patients could not escape. Although she arrived with a suitcase of her clothes, my grandmother's belongings started to go missing. *This happens,* a nurse explained to my dad, *they get confused, wander into each other's rooms, and take each other's clothes.*

The first time I visited her in the residence, I found my grandmother wearing a nightgown at four o'clock in the afternoon and a pair of shoes I had never seen before.

I blinked back tears as she struggled to place me. In her room, I sifted through her closet. There were items I didn't recognize, folded T-shirts and pants that belonged to other people. I texted my dad, upset to see the state of her half-empty closet. *They're just things,* he responded.

On the bottom shelf, I found a pile of familiar sweaters. I held one up and inspected it closely. I could practically see her, standing at the kitchen counter in the green knit cardigan, asking if I wanted a cup of tea. In the middle of the pile, I spotted a blue-and-pink striped blouse that I instantly recognized. It had been a birthday gift from my family twenty-five years earlier. Our birthdays were one day apart, and my grandmother and I always celebrated together. As I touched the soft fabric, I was flooded with happy memories. I held the shirt close before putting it back where she had hidden it.

Maybe clothes are just things. We can use them to hide, and eventually outgrow them. But they are also heirlooms, relics of a feeling and moment in time. As I stepped into my identity as a sober woman, learning how to dress was an exercise in self-respect and grace. Standing in front of my grandmother's closet, I said a quiet thanks to her clothes; they were the last anchor her memory had left.

From her chair by the window, my grandmother took me in, her eyes searching mine urgently. *My head is empty, but I know you,* she finally said in French when I sat back down next to her and took her hand.

I pulled out my phone and started showing her photos of relatives: my late grandfather, my dad and uncle, my brother.

She struggled with their names and invented rambling stories about how she knew them. When I got to a picture of me, she paused. *That's me,* she said definitively, pointing at my face. My smile was hers; her features were mine. In all my crises of confidence, the years spent comparing myself to other girls, I had forgotten a key part of my identity. I am my grandmother's granddaughter, the next chapter of her story. I wear her quiet confidence, her elegance, her love of family, no matter what outfit I have on.

Then she looked up at me and beamed. *I love your dress.*

11

'Tis the Season to Be Drunk

According to my dog's trainer, January 1 and July 5 are the most populated days of the year at animal shelters. The crowds consist of worried owners searching for their pets, scared dogs who ran away during festive fireworks the night before. I relate to those dogs.

Holiday noise always sent me running. From myself, from my life, from the reminder that another year had come and gone, and I was in the exact same place. I was single and aimless and these festivities were an excuse to escape wrapped in a bow. There were the big ones: Christmas, Thanksgiving, Valentine's Day, Halloween, the Fourth of July. I drank spiked cider and mulled wine at winter holiday parties, mystery punch at Halloween mixers, and red, white, and blue Jell-O shots at Fourth of July barbecues.

Celebration absolved me from the rules of consumption.

I feigned enthusiasm about the holidays, but a single refrain—
more—ran through my head. More drinks, more parties, more
justification for an entire month of hangovers. I smudged
lipstick on cocktail napkins and strangers' collars, slurring my
plea. Let's go to another bar, let's take one more shot, let's stay
out all night. *It's only (insert holiday here) once a year.*

The occasions themselves didn't matter; every event
was an excuse to drink, take a picture in a costume, and
wait for the Instagram likes to pour in. I hated being alone,
so I lost myself in holiday crowds. I blacked out on Saint
Patrick's Day, Cinco de Mayo, Memorial Day, Labor Day,
Easter, and Presidents' Day. I wore costumes, beads, themed
colors, knee socks, and too much eye shadow, the worn
soles of my Converse party sneakers thumping down city
sidewalks. My twenties felt heavy, and holiday weekends
provided the relief I so desperately craved; the permission
to sate my unquenchable thirst.

Alcohol was a firework ripping into my body, lighting
me up like a dark sky and sending me running into the
night.

* * *

WHEN I WAS six or seven, my parents hosted a holiday party
in our home. I wore a red plaid dress, tights, and shiny pat-
ent leather shoes. The guest list mostly included my dad's
coworkers and my parents' friends, but you would have
thought Santa Claus himself was attending. I flitted excitedly around the house all afternoon as my mom cleaned,
polished, and decorated the house. I snuck salty cashews

from little glass bowls of mixed nuts, following my mom from room to room and inspecting her handiwork. Nat King Cole began to croon from the stereo as the guests arrived, and I greeted everyone proudly with my dad. As the room filled, I was transfixed by the scene. Holiday parties, I decided, were magic. My house had never looked so beautiful, and I was allowed to dance, shoes and all, on the living room table.

The following year, I became obsessed with nosebleeds. I wasn't getting them, but kids in my class were. With nosebleeds came attention and a trip to the nurse's office, and I envied classmates on the receiving end of both. Still, my nostrils wouldn't cooperate. I watched in awe as my friends' tiny noses began to pour, inexplicably, blood pooling on their desks. I loved the theatrics of it all, but my nose wouldn't cooperate. I began to take matters into my own hands. I practiced at home, dragging my fingernails across my nostrils, pressing down harder until my septum began to bleed. The blood quantity was always disappointing; I wanted a flood and all I could produce were droplets. When my mom caught me in the act, she leveled with me: if I didn't stop giving myself nosebleeds, there would be no Christmas party that year. It shook me to my core. I needed the party; it was the most fun I had ever had.

I was raised Jewish and attended Hebrew School at a reform synagogue until my bat mitzvah. But still, I loved Christmas. I loved the twinkling lights, the music, and the *Frosty the Snowman* reruns. I felt out of place wherever I went: my brain and body were both betraying me. I wasn't

French or American enough, needed a sports bra by fifth grade, and struggled to fit in with the other girls. But Christmas culture was merry and inviting. I wanted to be right in the middle of it, a candy cane in pre-pubescent, human form.

I loved the holiday season even more when I started to drink. The magic I picked up on as a child was amplified with spiked cider. Anything was possible at Christmas, all the movies promised, and alcohol and I were on the hunt for a miracle.

* * *

THE YEAR I moved to New York City I lived in an apartment on top of a bagel store and across the street from a Duane Reade. My Midtown West zip code lacked charm, but it was within walking distance from the Rockefeller Center Christmas tree. I took the long way home most nights that winter, letting myself be carried by the throngs of tourists hoping to catch a glimpse of the holiday tree. New York was lonely, and that tree felt like a place of worship: a safe space for lost souls. I stood silently, transfixed by the spruce, taking a respectful, blurry picture every time I visited. I hoped I was absorbing whatever Christmas magic lingered in the air, charged holiday particles that might imbue me with an elf-like dose of cheer.

Cheer came in the form of SantaCon, a "holiday" primarily observed by recent college graduates in cities across the country. In New York, the festivities typically started in Murray Hill or Lower East Side apartment pre-parties before spilling into the streets. Technically, SantaCon is a holiday-themed bar crawl. In practice, it's an excuse for twenty-somethings to drink heavily at 11:00 AM in Santa suits.

In retrospect, I understand that SantaCon is embarrassing and awful. It's a day New Yorkers dread, a sloppy assault on city sidewalks and subways. But at twenty-two, I was excited. It had been two months since Halloween, the last time I had been given an excuse to devote an entire day to drinking in a disguise. I ordered my Santa suit online and made plans to get ready with friends.

I gasped when we walked into the sprawling Chelsea apartment. The loft—with its outdoor space and staircase—belonged to a friend's older brother and was a far cry from the starter apartments we were all cramming our miniskirts into. Michael was a few years ahead of us at Brown and had three roommates, all of whom had fancy finance and private equity jobs. Their apartment was packed with alumni wearing Santa hats and reindeer ears. For a moment I felt intimidated, but in the kitchen, we found life rafts: bagels, orange juice, and a full bar. We began to pour ourselves screwdrivers, mimosas, Baileys Irish Cream. It was 8:30 AM and we were ready to celebrate.

I started to drink, and as always, the alcohol had an enhancing effect. My blemishes were erased, my boots were unscuffed, my teeth were whitened. A few drinks later, I owned the place. The apartment was packed with bodies, and my friends and I made our rounds, taking group pictures on the balcony, in the kitchen, outside the bathroom. We cracked open Pabst Blue Ribbons and helped ourselves to circulating trays of green and red Jell-O shots. I inspected a picture of myself on my iPhone, illuminated in a sea of red Santas, and thought I had never looked prettier.

My friends and I had only graduated from college seven months earlier, but we were all pretending to be grown-ups. Our jobs were great, we lied. My party line was that I was working as a freelance writer and social media consultant while I chipped away at the novel I had started as my college thesis. The reality was that I had never finished my thesis, struggled to get out of bed most mornings, and went to therapy twice a week. We all had secrets.

By 11:00 AM, we started to take vodka shots. Holiday music swelled. Our hugs were getting longer, our smiles loopier, our bodies looser. We were so happy to see each other, we slurred, and we meant it. Time sped up and within an hour we were on the move, a herd of sloppy Santas headed down Sixth Avenue. In later years, I would grimace when I saw a mob of Santas rounding the corner. But at the time, being one of them was an honor.

Our destination was Peter McManus, a family-run Irish pub and New York City institution, operating since 1936. We descended upon the bar briefly, a sea of arms and dollar bills ordering frothy pints of beer, before moving to the next stop on our crawl. I allowed myself to move with the pack, never questioning where we were headed or how we were getting there. Someone else was always leading the way and it was a tremendous relief.

The final stop on our tour was a Spanish-style tapas

restaurant that our group had rented out for the day. Our entertainment was a musician named Dave Binder who performed at Brown every year at Spring Weekend, arriving with an acoustic guitar and serenading drunk undergraduates with his renditions of childhood and singalong songs like "Head, Shoulders, Knees, and Toes" and "Sweet Caroline." The result was a nostalgic and ritualistic showing of screams, cheers, and tears. The group had contacted Dave Binder and booked his services for SantaCon, and we danced around the restaurant happily, lapping up our beers and swaying with our arms around each other to "Jingle Bell Rock." My friend's ex-boyfriend slurred that he had always had feelings for me before abruptly leaving to meet another girl. I took a series of photos with a girl I had never spoken to but decided I had to befriend. By 2:00 PM I blacked out.

This was how every holiday should be spent, I decided as the light in my brain went out.

* * *

THE IDEA OF a sober holiday sounded anything but merry. In the weeks leading up to my first Halloween, Christmas, New Year's Eve without alcohol, I started waking up in the middle of the night with anxiety. My eyes would pop open at 3:00 AM, the glowing number on my phone reminding me of all the nights I was still out at this hour. As I watched the clock tick forward, my mind raced. Each millisecond meant I was getting closer to celebrating something sober, a sentence I had never said before.

For my first sober Halloween, I went to a party at a friend's apartment in downtown Manhattan. I still felt awkward and unsexy without alcohol, so I bought a costume that felt fitting for my mood: a hooded sloth onesie. *Wear it as pajamas and sleep like a cub,* the website suggested, and I considered sleeping through the whole holiday. My friends and I had dinner before the party, and I loaded up on French fries and Diet Coke to overcompensate for the calories I would not be drinking that night. For some reason, I believed *you deserve it* was synonymous with making myself feel sick. When we got to the party, I parked myself in a corner with a bowl of candy. Outside, the city purred as the parade flowed through the streets, a sea of cat ears and bodysuits shutting down Sixth Avenue. I felt like all eyes were on me as I turned down a sugary mixed drink and stifled a yawn. The holiday spirit was making me tired— and a little nauseous.

Sober Christmas wasn't much better. At work, we were gearing up for the big holiday party that a new hire was planning with the founders. One of the founders at my startup had decided the goal was to get everyone drunk. He was thoughtful in his approach. *I think,* he explained as we walked to get coffee one winter afternoon, *it's important for me to drink the most so I can lead by example. This way no one will feel uncomfortable letting loose.* I bought a new black dress and invited my old roommate Nina to be my plus-one.

I won't be drinking, I explained when I invited her over text message. And the girl planning it keeps saying things like 'we're gonna throw down' and 'it's gonna be lit,' which is like a lot even by normal standards.

She agreed to join for emotional support. The night of the party, I watched as my coworkers morphed from affable employees into party animals, hitting the makeshift dance floor in our basement office with the kind of gusto reserved for raves. When the co-founders made their way into the middle of the room with a bottle of tequila and began pouring it into employees' mouths, I pretended they'd already served me. I checked my phone anxiously. Where was Nina?

She arrived two hours later with a couple of friends. *The playlist sucks,* she informed me flatly. For some reason, I felt personally responsible for this. I spent the next hour dancing awkwardly, skirting tequila hits, and apologizing to Nina for the inadequate vibes. I left early; when I walked outside, it had started to snow.

The next day, another friend texted to see how the party was. It was objectively not fun, and I hid in the bathroom multiple times. But I am so happy I'm not hungover today. It wasn't much, but it was enough.

In the movies, the holiday season is a time to tell the truth, fall in love, and make out in the snow. I spent my first sober holiday season watching movies with my parents and cousins, eating cheese, and avoiding parties. The thought of standing in the middle of a room, stone-cold sober, while people coupled up to kiss at midnight around me was too unpleasant to imagine. I rang in that new year clinging to my sobriety and with very little holiday cheer to spare. There were some experiences I found surprisingly fun when I was newly sober: dancing, concerts, vacations. The holidays were not one of them. But that wouldn't always be the case.

* * *

WHEN I TURNED down a drink at Rosh Hashanah dinner, my dad raised his eyebrows. It would be another month before I told my parents the truth about my decision to quit drinking altogether, but in that moment, I just waved off the wine and loaded my plate with challah bread.

I had never drunk heavily around my dad. In his presence, I still felt like a teenager who needed to hide the fact that she had ever gotten drunk or kissed a boy. I wanted him to be proud of me: in home videos, I stood still, small and studied, ready to perform the poem or song I had most recently memorized. My younger brother, Eric, is just out of frame, racing around the house like a Tasmanian devil, free to be the kid of the house. But I feel so much older, so much more aware of my parents' reactions. My tiny voice is often heard repeating the same question: *Did I do a good job, Daddy?* It's funny, and a little tragic.

My dad grew up in Paris and brought European sensibilities to the way he parented us. He spoke to my brother and me directly, without baby talk. When JonBenét Ramsey was murdered in 1996, I was six—the same age she had been—and I had questions. My dad told me the truth: she had been strangled and found in her basement. *She doesn't have to know everything,* my mom exclaimed as my young face went slack with horror. But my dad didn't know any other way.

He brought the same no-nonsense approach to alcohol. My brother and I were both allowed small sips of whatever was on the table—beer, champagne, or zinfandel wine— like my father had been in France. Our favorite drink was a Panaché, a refreshing mix of beer and *limonade* (which is not lemonade but closely resembles 7UP) that my dad had been drinking at home since he was a child and or- dering for himself in restaurants since fifteen or sixteen. Like everything else he touched, my dad was measured and logical when it came to drinking. He could have a glass of wine with lunch on a Saturday afternoon and then settle in for an afternoon nap, like my grandfather had done before him.

I process alcohol differently. I tried to intellectualize it for years—maybe it was because I was brought up in America, with a different dialogue around alcohol and a higher legal drinking age. Maybe if I had been raised in Paris, maybe if I had been less anxious as a child, maybe, maybe, maybe. But the fact remained that when I drank, I did it differently than my dad. My lack of sophistication was shameful.

When I told my dad I was giving up alcohol altogether, he asked if I was overreacting a bit. He was ruled by science and troubled by extremes. *Why can't you just have one glass and then stop?* It wasn't a decision he could relate to, and that broke my heart. I wanted him to understand me, to see himself in me, to tell me I was doing the right thing.

Of course, he also didn't know the extent of my drinking and the situations I found myself in once alcohol took hold. The more he learned, the quieter his questions became. And when I celebrated three years sober, he told me he was proud of me.

My first sober Thanksgiving, my younger brother flew from California to New York for the holiday. I had been waiting to tell him about my sobriety in person, unsure of how he might react. Eric had been the fun one when we were kids and had continued to live on his own terms as we entered adulthood. Where I was controlled and obsessed with appearing perfect, Eric rejected societal expectations. He had moved across the country for college, deleted his social media accounts, grown his hair long, and been honest with my parents about smoking weed.

Even though Eric was now an adult, I still felt a deep need to be a model big sister to him. In my mind, this meant never admitting weakness, being the perfect mix of fun and successful, getting straight *A*'s and still knowing where all the good parties were happening. When he visited me in college years earlier, we had clinked our beers together and smiled for pictures. I thought of myself as an exemplary older sister, but the truth was likely somewhere in the middle. I was so consumed with taking care of him that I robbed him of a nonjudgmental sibling. Instead of walking through experiences with him, I grabbed him by the hand

and dragged him along, even when I had no idea where we were going. At holiday dinners, even if I wasn't drunk, I was dominating. I talked nonstop, told my stories, and elicited laughs from our parents. Eric sat, quiet and listening, never once interjecting. Sometimes I wondered if, deep down, he resented me, though he always swore he didn't. If I were him, I would have. When he called me from college to confess that he had gotten a tattoo and asked me not to tell our parents, I told my mom within an hour. I wanted to be his sister, but I also wanted to protect him and be a good daughter. I didn't know how to do all three.

Disclosing my struggles to Eric felt like chipping away at a wall I hadn't realized was between us. I invited him to my apartment in Brooklyn a few days before Thanksgiving, and we sat on my couch eating takeout. I was in sweats and no makeup, my hair pulled back and feet tucked underneath me. He listened intently, then thanked me for telling him the truth. He was there for me, he promised, no matter what. I felt very young, and as I looked at my brother, I realized how much we had both been hiding from each other. I told him about my blackouts, and he talked about his recent struggles with what felt like depression. In the years that followed, his battle with depression became more intense. I was desperate to fix it, to control and tell him what to do and where to go so he could feel better. But, like my drinking, I had spent years doing it my way. Now, I decided I would try practicing the opposite.

In sobriety, when we gathered for holiday dinners, I still

found myself itching to play the old part I had cast myself in three decades ago. I wanted to sparkle like the Christmas lights, but I tried sitting still instead. I let my brother take up space, and I didn't try to control him. I drank my water as my dad drank his wine, and I helped my mom in the kitchen. In time I realized that the warmth of my family's love still glowed, even when I wasn't at the center of it.

* * *

MY FIRST SANTACON didn't end as splendidly as it started. When I came out of my blackout, I was lying on my friend Sarah's couch, still wearing my Santa suit. It had gotten dark outside, and people had ordered food. I found a half-eaten Chipotle bowl at my feet when I got up to leave.

I tried to hail a cab, but drivers swerved to avoid me, a still-drunk Santa with a purse. I walked for twenty blocks until I realized I was in Times Square. The sight of the bright lights suddenly sent my stomach lurching: I tumbled into a trash can and promptly threw up. Elmo bumped into me as he moved to take pictures with tourists.

I replayed this memory during my first two sober holiday seasons whenever the urge to chug mulled wine started creeping in. I wanted to be the girl who sipped on Christmas cocktails underneath the mistletoe, but my old holiday stories bore a simple lesson. My drinking was never cute, and no amount of tinsel would change that.

Once I stopped idealizing boozy festivities, I realized my circumstances could only improve without alcohol. I also accepted that certain holidays, like Halloween, might need to be taken down a notch. Instead of dressing up in different costumes every night of the week leading up to Halloween, I relegated myself to normal human status: one costume, one party, one bag of candy. When I started dating someone in my second year sober, we spent Halloween together watching scary movies and eating mini candy bars. I was surprised to find it was one of the most fun Halloweens I had had in years.

Holidays sans booze continued to get more fun as I became more comfortable with myself. The desire to escape and disguise started to dissipate and made room for tiny moments of joy. They weren't the over-the-top celebratory variety I had always strived to create when I was drinking; these were simpler. I leaned into childhood traditions like putting out pumpkins in the fall, lighting the menorah at Hanukkah, and watching *Frosty the Snowman.*

On my third sober New Year's, I woke up on a Caribbean island with my boyfriend. I slipped out of bed as he slept and walked down to the ocean. The night before, we had celebrated the new year by eating mini hamburgers, blowing on noisemakers, and dancing until midnight. As the waves lapped at my feet, I smiled with the memory of how my heels had started to hurt the night before. I could still feel my toes aching. Someone had spilled a drink on my purse, and my bag still smelled vaguely like rum. In the pictures I looked a little sweaty, my hair frizzy, my smile lazy. But I remembered and felt it all, every tiny detail. I didn't want to lose myself in a crowd or hide behind a costume. This, I decided, must be holiday cheer.

12

On Mothers and Daughters

In 1997, the Spice Girls were important to me: they were teaching me about girl power, positivity, and friendship. I spent afternoons perched on the windowsill in my bedroom, my red cassette player in my lap, decoding every lyric. Which was how I learned about "Mama," one of the slow songs on their first album.

One morning, as my mom collected the laundry basket from my room, I decided to serenade her. I cued up the tape and pressed play, waiting patiently for her to stop and notice this love letter from daughters to mothers. I hoped it would make her happy.

She had been crying a lot recently. Later, I learned it was because her mom's breast cancer had returned, but at eight years old I worried it was because of me. I tried to be well-behaved, to help with my little brother and turn off the television when she called us for dinner. But I could feel the sadness leaking out of her, spilling onto my cheeks when she kissed me goodnight.

Mama, I love you, the Spice Girls sang. My mom didn't seem to register the lyrics, so I raised the volume slightly. *Mama, my friend.* My mom continued collecting dirty socks, unaware that I was trying to send her a message. On her way out of the room, she asked me to lower the music.

* * *

THE LINK BETWEEN my mom and me was always vulnerable, too tender to touch. As a little girl I knotted my fingers in her hair before bed, twisting the strands into my tiny fists so she would be unable to slip away once I was asleep. When my grandmother got sick again, I became desperate to cure my mom's grief, to fix what wasn't mine to mend. This is what we do as mothers and daughters. We pocket each other's pain, smoothing it over until it becomes our own stone to carry.

At seventeen, when I moved to New York City for college, I felt a sharp tug, the reminder that I was tethered to another human being who loved me so much it hurt. We both cried for weeks after I moved out, though I couldn't articulate why I felt so afraid to be far from her.

Homesickness, my college advisor sighed, bored, as I tore through a box of tissues in his office, *passes eventually.*

But my mom was the house I was sick over. I missed her hugs, and the way she popped her head into my room to check on me when I was up late doing homework. I worried about the distance between us. On walks home from class, I burst into tears at the sight of a mother and daughter together. I felt like a different person: in high school I had been passionate, cocky, the first one to raise my hand in class. Now I was lost, the quintessential little fish in a big pond, a child missing her mommy.

Drinking helped ease the transition between who I had been and who I might become. I felt less petrified—of the unknown, of forming new connections, of being apart from my mom—after drinking a vodka cranberry (or five). The morning after, depending on how my night had gone, I would either call my mom jubilant (*I made friends!*) or hungover. I never told her how much I drank, and she never asked. I think we were both relieved to find I was starting to settle in, that my well of tears seemed to be drying up. Life was what started to happen at parties, sandwiched into off-campus kitchens and dorm rooms, and alcohol was my guide. In time, it became my new security blanket, rocking me to sleep while my mom was miles away.

* * *

THREE YEARS AFTER I graduated from college, they found a lump in my mom's left breast.

Stage three breast cancer, my dad told me, describing what would happen next. There would be surgery, sixteen weeks of chemotherapy, and thirty rounds of radiation. When I dumbly asked if she would lose her hair, he looked away for a second. *I don't know,* he lied.

My dad had just started a new job and couldn't make

it to every appointment; my parents had just sold the New Jersey house where I had my first hangover, so I moved into their New York City apartment with them while I applied to graduate school. I became my mom's caretaker and companion, taking notes at oncologist appointments and asking the questions my mom couldn't remember once her chemo brain fog set in.

She did lose her hair. Eyebrows and lashes too. Sometimes I watched her sleep, her bare skull a sea of grooves. It reminded me of a dinosaur egg, a pale stretch of skin with a familiar face etched into the side. My most familiar face, the one I had always been so desperate to protect but could not shield from this. If life were a movie, this is the part where I would quit drinking and clean up my act. But my mom's diagnosis was the perfect excuse to drink even more. After hours in the chemo suite, I would tuck my mom into bed and go out in the city, my skin still smelling like hospital and bleach.

One winter night, I lost track of time. When I looked up, I realized a blizzard was underway outside and the bar had cleared. I had been so caught up in drinking and crying to a handsome stranger about my mom's diagnosis that I had missed my friends leaving just as the snow started coming down. I checked my phone and found a dozen messages from my mom, who had woken up at 2:00 AM to find I still wasn't home. As the snow continued piling up on the sidewalks, casting a quiet spell over the city, I walked alone for blocks until hailing a lone cab home. Another night, I got back to the apartment at 5:00 AM after blacking out and throwing up on myself at a party. I had made it all the way back home, only to pass out in the hallway outside the front door. I came to, keys clutched in my fist, purse open and hanging off my body. *My friend was having a bad night,* I lied when my mom asked me where I had been the next day.

My mom never questioned me, only hugged me before going back into her room. The effects of chemotherapy are cumulative, meaning they get worse with each round. My mom became weaker after every infusion, which meant I was able to creep into my room and nurse my hangovers while she rested, clueless about my drinking. The guilt was sickening, but I told myself I was protecting her from the truth. We never talked about what I did when I wasn't with her, and I did my best to shield her from what she couldn't fix, the broken parts of me that weren't hers to mend.

People told me I was strong when my mom was sick. They sent gift baskets, Chinese food, and T-shirts with phrases like *Being Fabulous Is the Best Comeback* and *Fuck Cancer!* I played the part of the organized daughter who could list her mom's medication schedule without needing to check my notes.

But I didn't feel strong. And I quickly developed a new understanding of why people drank: it wasn't just about having fun at parties. Alcohol was an effective antidote for the scary moments that felt too heavy to hold. *You deserve a drink,* friends told me when I talked about my mom's cancer. *Let yourself have some fun.* My world felt like it was collapsing, and I was desperate to escape. But even at my drunkest, the relief never came.

* * *

MY MOM'S CANCER was both shocking and not a surprise. Breast cancer runs in my family, the way laugh lines or chocolate cake recipes are passed down in others. I could only count as far back as my great-grandmother and great-aunt, both of whom had died from the big C.

Then there was my maternal grandmother, who was diagnosed with breast cancer the year I was born and spent the next twelve years of my life miserable. Even in the years she was in remission, she was never really healthy, always complaining of aches and pains. When we visited her in Maryland, she insisted that my younger brother and I go play at my cousins' house so she could be alone with my mom.

I ached for my mom during these afternoons; I didn't understand why my grandmother seemed so intent on separating us. Whenever I asked to stay, promising I would be quiet, my grandmother shook her head firmly. *She's sick, honey,* my mom offered as an explanation. *She doesn't want to upset you. Too late,* I always thought.

I felt uneasy around my grandmother, which isn't something you're supposed to say. I could feel the unspoken competition coursing between us, and it perplexed me. When I was eight, my grandparents came to stay with us for a week.

One night after dinner, my mom sat with me at the kitchen table, helping me with my homework. My grandmother put the tea kettle on, laying out two mugs and clearing her throat pointedly in our direction. She wanted me to go upstairs and get ready for bed so she could be alone with my mom, but I wasn't ready to concede.

I need help with my homework, I said stubbornly. School trumped cancer.

My grandmother sighed. *I'm always telling my friends how smart you are. But if you need so much help with your homework, maybe I've been wrong . . .*

Checkmate. She had me cornered. If there was anything I cared about more than winning a battle for my mom's attention, it was being the smartest one in class. I slammed my book shut and went upstairs to my room. No one followed me.

When my grandmother's cancer metastasized and spread to her bones four years later, I didn't know what to feel. My parents sat my brother and I down at the kitchen table to tell us when she died. I went upstairs and sank onto the floor, clamping a hand over my mouth so no one would hear me cry. It was the only time I cried over her death.

As my body changed and I grew breasts, I rejected them. I strapped them down in tight sports bras and drowned them in baggy T-shirts. I hid them from men and from myself. When a friend told me her boyfriend referred to me as *the girl with the great rack,* I bought an oversized coat. I hated what my breasts represented: excess fat and room for cancer cells to multiply. They were ticking time bombs strapped to my chest.

After my mom's diagnosis, she went in for genetic testing. I held her hand and watched the nurse prick needles into her veins. They were seafoam green, the same color as her eyes. *You're negative for BRCA,* the doctor told us, scanning her results like he was reading a lunch menu. *But it's possible, given your family history, that you have a different genetic mutation we haven't identified yet.* This was hardly comforting.

Over the next six months, I observed my mom's cancer protocol the way a prospective homeowner studies a house. I learned my way around the hospital, asked questions about the chemo drips, wrote down her side effects. One day, I joked, this would all be mine. It was easier to make dark jokes than admit I was terrified for both of us. Our family history loomed over me constantly, and my body felt like a temporary residence that might betray me at any second.

When I drank, I tried to evacuate my bones. I didn't trust my body, so I didn't care what happened to it. At a housewarming party with a cute lawyer who I had been set up with, I pounded glasses of sangria and watched the ceiling fan spin. The next thing I knew, his hand was on my back, pulling me in close. When I woke up in his bed the next morning, I couldn't remember if we had used a condom. Later that morning, I snuck out of my mom's chemo suite to slip the Plan B pill pack out of my purse and under my tongue. *Side effects may include breast tenderness,* the box warned.

A month later, I started to have panic attacks. They seized me in the shower, in my bed, as I got on the subway. I should have been relieved: my mom was almost finished with her course of treatment. We could see the light on the other side of the tunnel, the nurses liked to remind us. But I was always scared. I couldn't let myself trust our bodies. Not anymore.

* * *

I ONCE HEARD a young woman in a recovery meeting share that she drank to ward off what felt like a permanent home-sickness; a gaping hole in her chest that no amount of booze could fill. I drank for many reasons, but the home-sickness hypothesis resonated deeply with me the first time I heard it.

I had always struggled with transitions. I wept at my first slumber party until my mom arrived in her pajamas to bring me home. My mom was the antidote to my per-sistent homesickness; she made me feel safe.

She's too attached to you, I overheard my dad tell my mom once when I was in college. *You're not doing her any favors.* The tears were quick and hot, my face burning with em-barrassment.

Later, I understood that he was right: I was probably too attached to her. But I wasn't ashamed. Our bond kept me tethered to where I had come from. Her arms, her chest, her scars, were mine too.

My mom had a complicated upbringing. Her father, a liquor salesman in Manhattan, worked constantly, while her mother spent days in bed with what she called migraines and were likely depressive episodes. My mom was loved— she told me her parents did their best—but she lacked attention. Her older brother, who could be a bully, was often tasked with looking after her and her twin sister. As a little girl, I heard stories about my mom's childhood that upset me, like the time my uncle lifted her into the dryer, head-first, and held her body down as he turned the machine on. My mom remembers crying and feeling helpless as the dryer whirled around her.

I felt fiercely protective of my mom and the girl she had once been, and I developed the belief that I needed to take care of her. I eavesdropped on her phone conversations with her siblings to make sure nothing was being kept from me. I needed to keep tabs on all the situations at play to ensure my mom was safe. At seven, I was up to date on my aunt's latest divorce proceedings and custody hearings. I weighed in on the dynamics between her and her ex-husband and shook my head when she didn't demand he pay child support.

My desire to keep my mom safe could feel compulsive. When she was running late to pick me up from dance class or a friend's house I would panic, my chest tightening as I played horrible scenarios in my head. And when she was diagnosed, this line of thinking became all-consuming. To this day, it's challenging for me to articulate feelings of frustration toward my mom. I can fight with my husband, dad, and brother. But if my mom and I get close to arguing, I back down: I can't bear the thought of hurting her. It's partially for this reason that I was dishonest with her about my drinking. I would have done anything to protect my mom from worry or pain, including lying to her.

When I stopped drinking there was less to lie about. My whereabouts were accounted for, and I didn't have to make up explanations for lost phones and wallets. But I still found myself withholding the truth about past experiences from my mom, nights I knew she would replay in her head long after I had finished describing them.

My mom is my best friend: we speak multiple times a day and understand each other unlike anyone else can. But there was so much I kept from her. I wondered how many other mothers and daughters did the same, talking constantly without saying anything that might upset the other.

In my early years without alcohol, I started to think about the health of my relationships. When I shared my aversion to arguing with my mom in therapy, my therapist explained that true closeness can't exist without conflict.

People pleasing can actually be manipulative, she explained. *Because it's us trying to avoid conflict for ourselves.*

I could use whatever words I liked, but the truth was clear. Where I claimed to be protective, I was controlling. Where I cited agreeability, there was withholding. I wasn't looking to go out and start blowout fights, but I began to strive for total honesty with my mom, even if there was a chance it might upset her.

As our relationship continued to evolve in sobriety, it became fuller. I didn't tell her every little detail about what happened when I had been drinking, but I answered her questions honestly as they came up. We still didn't fight, but we rubbed up against disagreements about little things, like how many bully sticks she could give my dog, Brie, when she was watching her (one as a special treat only, and no human food). For me, this was progress. There is no one I love more than my mom, but there is also no one harder for me to disagree with or write about. I'm working on it. And at least, now, she knows.

* * *

TWO YEARS AFTER I stopped drinking, I made an appointment with a doctor who specialized in the prevention and early detection of breast cancer. I was a candidate for RISE, a program dedicated to treating individuals at an increased risk for breast cancer due to genetic predisposition and family history of the disease, but I had been putting off scheduling an appointment for years. As I filled out the intake paperwork on my laptop, my stomach did flips. I typed out the numbers I dreaded: how old my great-grandmother, great-aunt, grandmother, aunt, and mother had been when they were each diagnosed with cancer.

On the morning of the appointment, I bought myself an overpriced latte and got off the subway early so I could walk a few extra city blocks. It was a warm June day, and I was scared. I reminded myself of all the reasons I could do this. If I could get through a bachelorette party without alcohol, I could make it through this appointment. If I could sit through my ex-boyfriend's acoustic guitar renditions of Coldplay songs, I could survive a single conversation with a doctor. But I was still anxious. I didn't want to hear what the doctor had to say. I worried that between my drinking, genetics, and body, I was predestined for problems.

Still, I put one foot in front of the other, like sobriety had taught me to do. On my walk, I put my headphones in and cued up a '90s pop playlist. I relaxed as the bubblegum melodies started.

As I walked up to the office, my nerves settled. Because I didn't have to do this alone. There, waiting for me with a smile on her face and her new head of hair, was my mom, my home. We had survived her double mastectomy, three surgeries, and rounds of chemotherapy, and we would survive this. I reached out to take her hand, and the Spice Girls started singing our song.

PART IV

FREE

13

POV: You Have a POV

The year Lin-Manuel Miranda's *Hamilton* hit the Internet, I listened to the soundtrack religiously. I didn't pay for a premium Spotify account, so the songs played on shuffle with advertisements in between, which slightly slowed the plotline. Still, I understood the premise: the show followed Alexander Hamilton, an American Founding Father, on his ascent to political power. Alexander Hamilton, played by Miranda, was depicted as being hungry, motivated, and bright. He wrote like he was running out of time.

As I cobbled bits of the story together, I became obsessed. I played the music on the subway, while I got dressed for first dates, and on the elliptical. Like so many others, I was struck by Miranda's creativity and work ethic. I memorized the lyrics and began to see New York through Hamilton's eyes. The story stirred something in me, nudging me ever so slightly outside my monotonous routine and into the light. It inspired me to become someone other than who I was: a perpetually hungover twenty-six-year-old with zero direction. I tried to sit down at my laptop and write the next great American novel, but the words didn't come. I wanted to be bold and accomplished—I was living *in the greatest city in the world*—but all I thought about was partying. I wanted to lead by example, but I was a rule follower and people pleaser who craved approval.

Then, one day, it hit me: I wasn't Alexander Hamilton. I was Aaron Burr.

Jealous, obedient, fair-weathered Burr. *If you stand for nothing, Burr, what will you fall for?* Hamilton asks Burr early in the show. When I drank, I stood for nothing because I was down for whatever. Any restaurant, any bar, any after-party. I was always down for another round of shots, down to go back to your place and smoke, down for dancing. I did a lap at every party before committing to a location, sifting through conversations like playing cards, wondering if I was missing out on something cooler.

At parties I often pretended to be informed, nodding along as acquaintances ranted about politics, books, public policy. I couldn't believe how many people had a point of view. I wondered when they had the time to read, consider, and form a perspective. I didn't have room for informed opinions because I thought about myself constantly. I wondered what strangers thought about me, obsessed over my job title and appearance, and compared myself to everyone else. I was apathetic when it came to romantic interactions too. I saw dating as a metric for gauging my external appeal, versus a way to form a genuine connection with another human being. Sex was the ultimate victory: a sign that I was desired by someone, anyone. But in bed, I was a blank slate. The win had already been logged, so my preferences were sidelined.

My cool-girl alter ego was a liar: I was anxious, insecure, and trapped in a loop of self-centered thoughts. I hoped going with the flow would make everyone like me, and I hoped everyone liking me would make me like me.

When I became sober two years later, I still embodied a very Aaron Burr energy. I didn't want to make waves by not drinking, so I stayed out late even though I was tired and chipped in for alcohol I hadn't touched at parties. I dog-sat for free, went into the office on weekends, and said yes to every social invitation, even with people I wasn't sure I liked. I didn't trust myself, so I honored everyone else's preferences over my own.

* * *

THE YEAR I stopped drinking I went to see a new psychiatrist. I had been taking a low dose of Lexapro since college, and my internist had suggested I see someone to make sure the prescription was still the right fit for my anxiety. I was optimistic when I found a doctor with positive online reviews who accepted my health insurance and offered weekend hours.

When I sat down in his Upper East Side office on a Sunday, I scanned the room quickly. The requisite degrees were framed and hanging on his wall, and small frog figurines lined his bookshelf. He looked up from his computer screen to greet me and gestured for me to take a seat across from his desk. He was young, probably in his late thirties, with dark hair and glasses.

At his prompting, I told him a little bit about myself: my history with therapy, and how long I had been taking medication. When I mentioned I had quit drinking, he stopped typing and looked at me.

Like you're totally sober? What's that about?

I folded my hands in my lap and described the blackouts, the hangovers, and how I had tried to moderate my drinking unsuccessfully in the past. He looked unconvinced.

When was your last serious relationship?

I didn't follow the line of questioning, but I answered anyway. I told him I had been in a serious relationship for most of college but had trouble forming intimate connections with emotionally available men. I figured he would be impressed with my level of self-awareness.

Okay, so there was the guy in college, and then who else? How long has it been?

Was he making a timeline? I cleared my throat. I had gone on plenty of first, second, even third, and fourth dates. I had hookup buddies and guys who texted me late at night. I had found bits of physical connection and emotional compatibility, but not in the same package. Not in six years.

His eyes widened like I had just confessed to murder.

Jesus Christ! he exclaimed. He was deadly serious. He began typing quickly. *That isn't right. We need to get you in here at least twice a week and get down to the bottom of this. A pretty girl like you should have a boyfriend.*

I was stunned. Sometimes, when men made outrageous comments to my face, I simply froze.

The same thing had happened on a first date a couple of years earlier, when a divorcé I met on Bumble put down his second dirty martini to remark that I was *so much prettier in person* than in my photos. I laughed along, too shocked to muster up an authentic reaction in real time. When he pulled out my dating profile and started giving commentary on each one of my photos (*In this one, your nose looks big. This one is a weird angle. This just isn't a great picture . . .*), I sat very still and nodded along, like I was grateful for the constructive feedback.

Sitting across from the psychiatrist, I found myself repeating the same pattern. I nodded in agreement; he was the expert, the one in charge. I was obedient, Aaron Burr incarnate. I booked an appointment for the following week and left the office feeling unsettled.

But as I walked along the city sidewalks, something strange happened. I heard a voice inside of me that sounded a little bit like a point of view. The psychiatrist may have had fancy degrees and a sprawling uptown office, but I didn't agree with his professional opinion. I may have been incredibly single, but I was healing. Something in my gut told me I was going to be okay, and I believed it. I canceled my follow-up appointment with him the next morning and never saw him again.

As I became more comfortable with myself, I realized something revolutionary: being *down* was not a personality trait. In fact, it was kind of boring. I thought about Alexander Hamilton. He made enemies everywhere he went, but he didn't care. Burr, on the other hand, played it safe and wound up the villain in our history books. Being liked by everyone was literally impossible. As I began to accept that, I started to feel a little bit freer. Slowly, I inched toward establishing real preferences.

* * *

EIGHTEEN MONTHS LATER, I was still practicing having a point of view. I said no to movies about outer space, preferred eating dinner before 9:00 PM, and requested that people take their shoes off when they got to my apartment. Every time I discovered a new preference, I felt a tiny glimmer of pride. I had more work to do when it came to unfamiliar subjects. My instinct, like Aaron Burr, was still to pretend I knew it all. But when I fell in love as a sober woman, I collided into another world I knew nothing about.

One morning, on a trip to Montauk at the start of our relationship, Adam and I went for a walk on the beach. As the waves washed ashore and we sipped on hot coffee in paper cups, Adam grabbed my arm.

Look! Something small was creeping across the sand,

toward the water. I stared at him blankly. *Haven't you ever seen a baby turtle before?* he asked.

It was possible I had crossed paths with one before, but I had no memory of it. The old me would have nodded, feigning familiarity. Instead, I crouched down to take a closer look.

Adam spouted off facts: sea turtles lived in the water, he said, but lay their eggs on dry land. After laying the eggs, they embarked on a journey from their nest back into the water. I wondered, for the first time in my life, if sea turtles felt tired after giving birth. *What happens to its eggs? How do they survive?* I asked Adam. I studied the tiny creature, intuitively making its way back to the ocean. Later, it occurred to me that I would have missed the wonder of the moment entirely had I pretended to already know about it.

The following month, we went blueberry picking in Maine. When I peeled my sweatshirt off after an hour of picking berries off bushes, my skin was warm, and my fingers were stained blue. I had no idea that fruits start as flowers, I texted my mom that afternoon. Something to do with bees and pollination?? I never looked at a blueberry the same way again.

Adam, my nature guide, dragged me out of bed late at night, insisting I follow him out onto the beach to see the night sky. I pulled my sweatshirt around me, slightly annoyed. I had seen stars before. But it turned out I hadn't seen them like this. Unencumbered by light pollution, the sky was darker than I had ever seen, the stars impossibly bright. I gasped, and looked over to find Adam watching me, grinning. *Orion's Belt,* he explained, pointing.

In the years I spent drinking, I existed in a contained universe: I was either thinking about myself or wondering how people saw me. I didn't have space for opinions, preferences, or absorbing the beauty of the natural world around me.

Looking for Orion's Belt is the easiest way to locate Orion in the night sky, I read in bed on my phone.

As I turned over to fall asleep, I thought of the sea turtle making its way back to the ocean, and that strip of stars in the velvet night sky. I didn't know what I didn't know, and it was a wonderful, hopeful feeling. When I pretended to be a walking encyclopedia, unfazed by anything, I missed out on tiny, beautiful moments. As my world view continued to expand, my perspective shifted along with it.

* * *

Two years later, I was about to pick a familiar fight.

I was well-versed in having an opinion now. But sometimes, I wished I could go back to the way it was before I had such strong preferences.

It always started the same way: Adam reached to pour himself another glass of wine or ordered another cocktail at dinner, and I flinched. Logically, I knew he was allowed to drink however much he wanted. He wasn't the one who blacked out or couldn't stop once he started. And yet, I felt the urge to control him. An opinion rose in me, my voice spilling out like chardonnay into a goblet.

Are you sure you want another? I hated how I sounded. When I was drinking, I would have been furious if someone had questioned my intake. I even swiped *no* on dating apps when people described themselves as casual drinkers. I wanted to be with people who partied like I did. So how, now, had I become the alcohol police?

He groaned.

I'm not judging, I said defensively, clearly judging. *I just don't know why you need to have another one.*

I knew it wasn't fair, but the devil on my shoulder was indignant: it was my opinion, my finely tuned perspective, that he should stop drinking after one or two glasses. So why couldn't I let my opinion be known?

There was a quieter voice in my head too. I knew Adam drank. He had never pretended otherwise. He had even asked me on our first date if it was a problem for me, which it wasn't. I genuinely wasn't bothered by the sight of cocktails at dinners or tequila shots at weddings and birthday parties. My sobriety had nothing to do with how other people drank. So why was I picking at him now?

I called a friend who had been sober for nine years. I was hoping she would tell me what I wanted to hear: I was right, and Adam was wrong. I wanted confirmation that his drinking was supposed to change now that we were living together. I wanted her to tell me I could control him.

Instead, she told me the truth. *You're entitled to your feelings. But sometimes, just because we feel something, doesn't mean we need to share it with that person.*

I had a perspective and opinion—*you should stop drinking*

because I can't do it anymore—but it wasn't necessarily fair. Adam had always been supportive of my recovery and respectful when it came to drinking around me. Now, I had to admit that my reaction was not about him. It was rooted in my own feelings: anxiety, discomfort, and, yes, slight jealousy that he could drink and I couldn't.

It wasn't just Adam's drinking that I noticed. I was obsessed with the way everyone in my life drank. I paid attention to every cocktail my friends ordered at dinner. I wondered how specific people felt the morning after drinking at a wedding, and I had opinions about it. Being around alcohol wasn't a trigger for me; I was fascinated by it. Living in close quarters with someone who drinks helped me to understand that the way other people drank was none of my business. It had nothing to do with them, and everything to do with me. In this instance, my perspective was one I could keep to myself.

That day on the phone, my friend shared the three questions she asked herself before sharing her opinion with someone. *Was it true? Was it kind? Was it necessary?* I committed the questions to memory and began bringing them into other areas of my life too.

Before I quit drinking, I loved the taste of gossip on my tongue. It got me high, filling me with a sense of self-importance and value. But it began to lose its luster as I spent more time sober. Without alcohol in my stomach, gossip had a nauseating effect, like eating something too sweet. When I got caught repeating a rumor a friend had told me in confidence, I swore gossip off for good. Just because I had opinions now, it didn't mean I had to share them with everyone.

*   *   *

A YEAR LATER, at dance lessons before our wedding, Adam and I got in trouble. We hadn't practiced enough, and it showed. *I have eight-year-olds who can waltz better than you,* our instructor scowled. I counted box steps and rock steps and spins on counts of eight, stumbling in the heels I had been instructed to wear. *One, two, three, four, five, six, seven, eight.* Our instructor sent us home with a video recording where we looked awkward, stiff.

A lot of things are better without alcohol. Food, sex, travel. Learning to waltz isn't one of them.

I wished, just for a second, that I could glide through this dance after a glass of wine.

Don't forget to tilt your head all the way back, our instructor shouted through her Eastern European accent as she walked us through the waltz-into-lift-into-dip transition. I tried to interrupt; I wasn't even sure Adam would be able to lift me in my dress. *You must practice. Dance is most important part of wedding.*

She was serious. When you are getting married, everyone tells you their area of expertise is *the most important part of a wedding.* My dentist shamed me for not having my teeth professionally whitened. My esthetician urgently begged me to wax my forearms. My therapist told me to book more sessions. Now, standing in the dance studio with three weeks until the wedding, I wasn't sure I could handle one more *most important part.*

When I was drinking, I worried about my hypothetical wedding from time to time. Not the dress or the venue, but how I would be able to survive an open bar coupled with the pressure of the biggest night of my life without blacking out. There was no way I wouldn't have been a drunk bride. I knew I would be drinking before, during, and after the wedding. I often envisioned steeling myself through my vows, focusing on not slurring, and rewarding myself with a giant drink at cocktail hour before tripping over my own feet during my first dance. I always shook these thoughts away, shuddering. *Future me will figure that out,* I would think as I reached for another glass of wine.

Now, my future self was in the driver's seat. I was not in danger of blacking out and spoiling the day for myself and my husband. But I was still worried about stumbling through our first dance.

Then, it hit me. I didn't get sober to trip over my feet. I was a present, active participant in all aspects of my life, and that included my first dance.

I wanted to make our dance instructor proud; authority figures and teachers were my favorite people to please. But I had also been working on forming my own opinions, listening to them, and trusting myself enough to know when and where to share them. As I watched Adam look at me nervously in the dance studio, I took a deep breath.

Karolyna, I began slowly. *I think we need to start from scratch. The routine is too complicated.*

Her brow furrowed; she wasn't happy. In fact, she was disappointed. She paced around the room, and I wondered if we should leave. But eventually, she listened. She simplified the choreography, and I felt myself relax. And as Adam and I slowly danced around our living room that night, practicing the elementary routine she had reluctantly taught us, I smiled to myself.

In time, I realized that having a perspective didn't just impact my interpersonal relationships; it also affected how I interacted with the world. When it came to informing myself about current events and social issues, I had always borrowed outside opinions. I parroted what I heard at home or on television, too lazy to discover what I really believed. And even in sobriety, I used my drinking as an excuse for my ignorance. *I spent years focused on partying,* I told myself. *And the news is so triggering.* But eventually, I realized I had a responsibility to use my voice and sober brain for good. If I had the time to discuss the cultural impact of the Real Housewives franchise, I could start developing a broader perspective on the world around me. I started to read more, ask questions about what I didn't understand, and listen.

I thought I was so easygoing when I was drinking, but I just didn't have enough faith in myself to speak my mind. In sobriety, I discovered, adjusted, and accepted my preferences. I practiced saying them out loud and got to know myself through my point of view. I noticed the birds and the trees, and I also paid attention to how people made me feel. And when I stopped worrying about winning everyone else over, I started to win over myself. I felt powerful every time I formed and honored my own opinion. Having a point of view and knowing when to use it was a dance of its own, but I was getting better at learning the steps. Maybe I had a little Alexander Hamilton in me, after all.

14

My Social Media Archives

It just feels like I'm not cool enough for your curated feed, said my friend Hailey. She had just noticed that I had removed several photos of the two of us from my Instagram profile.

I could tell she was hurt, but I didn't know what to say. I was twenty-seven, single, and obsessed with curating my online persona. I saw life as one big potential photo opportunity. I forced my friends to take group photos at every bar and birthday dinner, throwing my arms over their shoulders with what I hoped was a carefree and fun energy. As soon as the picture was taken, I grabbed my phone and retreated into it, zooming in on my arms, face, and smile. *Can we take another one?* I inevitably begged my friends.

Once I settled on the best angles, facial expression, and composition, I started working on a filter, then edited my body on apps designed to minimize silhouettes. I pinched my waist, whitened my teeth, and erased my pimples. Next, the caption: I had to strike a balance between clever, thoughtful, and detached. After adding a few emojis, it was time to post. My friends tried to pull me out of my digital world and back into theirs, where they were talking about getting a promotion or fighting with a parent. But my phone felt hot in my hand; I couldn't stop checking it. As I waited to see how well a post would perform, I felt empty. I relished the hit of dopamine that coursed through my body, calming me, as I watched the likes start rolling in.

Back in my Brooklyn apartment, I lost track of time in my phone. Sprawled out on my bed, I inspected my profile from all angles, studying old posts. But in the right light, everything looked wrong. I tore through my profile with a digital machete, rewriting captions and deleting pictures that made me look too basic, boring, or overeager. I had done this to my Facebook profile years earlier, deleting all my old profile pictures before transferring colleges so I could control my new friends' first impressions of me. It turned out that not having any old profile pictures made for a bizarre first impression, but I didn't learn that until later.

Many of us were addicted to social media to some extent; we feasted on likes and followers, got high off validation in the palm of our hands. Much like I tried to take breaks from my drinking, I put myself on social media timeouts. But they never lasted long. My fingers itched for my phone, involuntarily swiping up for Instagram, where I felt safest. I dreamed in grids, viewed life as a series of interactions I could post about. My friends joked that I was their go-to for questions about writing captions or selecting pictures for dating apps. I lived online and was fluent in swiping.

Then one night, I discovered the Archive feature. Archiving allowed users to hide old posts without permanently deleting them. For many, archiving a photo was innocent. Companies archived posts that didn't match a new brand aesthetic; some people simply changed their mind about posting in the first place. *Felt cute, might delete later.* But I archived differently. It was my version of cutting bangs post-breakup, instantly altering my outsides when my insides were writhing. When my best friend erased me from her real life because I was drinking too much, I archived any trace of her from my online one. When I posted a sunset alongside a vulnerable caption about my anxiety, it barely hit fifty likes. I archived it so swiftly, it was like it never happened. I imagined the sun rising back into the sky in reverse, obliterating the memory of my words.

With archiving, I could drunkenly post a selfie from a bar, hide it when I inevitably decided I hated it, and bring it back later if I changed my mind. I archived my Instagram profile the way some people clean out their closets. If a post hadn't sparked joy in the last year, I removed it. Unlike in real life, my digital personality was malleable. I linked my Instagram account to my dating profiles, providing potential suitors with a deeper look into my personality. (Just kidding: all anyone cared about was swiping through more pictures.)

Here's a short play I wrote to illustrate the phenomenon of archiving:

FADE IN:
INT. MY LIVING ROOM – DAY

I sit on my couch, swiping mindlessly through my phone. After a few seconds, I place it on a table. Then, I stand up and hide my phone in my purse. I sit back on the couch, trying to relax, but my fingers itch for the device. My heart rate accelerates. A violin starts to play, quickening as the seconds tick by. There is a thrumming in my head that becomes impossible to ignore, much like a gnawing urge to pop a pimple. I know I shouldn't do it, but I also feel certain I will experience great relief if I do. I thrash on the couch, aching for the release of pressure in my chest. It's urgent now: if I can just fix my grid, archive my old pictures, get more likes, and manipulate my digital footprint, everything will be okay. The music crescendos. I stand to reach for my phone and descend into madness.

CUT TO BLACK. THE END.

If you've never experienced a social media binge, this might sound silly. But being in the throes of one can feel a lot like a blackout. I could look up from my phone, suddenly thirsty and with a splitting headache, and find hours had passed. It was scary, powerful, and impossible to kick.

It wasn't just about looking cool, I wanted to tell Hailey. I didn't want to hurt her. But I couldn't stop. Archiving was power. It let me erase myself, scrubbing away all the parts I hated until there was nothing left.

* * *

ONE SUNNY MORNING a year after I moved to Los Angeles, two police officers arrived at my apartment building. It was too early in the day for a noise complaint or a drunken domestic dispute. I was on the way out, and I lingered at my car for a few minutes too long, waiting for any potential drama. I had just gotten to the coffee shop where I liked to write when my phone rang.

They're here for a wellness check, Adam started talking as soon as I answered. It sounded like he was outside. *Do you know anyone named Elizabeth?*

I furrowed my brow. Our building was small, only eight units, and we knew most of our neighbors by name. *No idea. Maybe she's the one who's always traveling?*

I wrote five sentences before my phone rang again. Adam's voice was different. *She never went by Elizabeth. It was Tibby.* He was talking too fast. *They found her inside. Can you come home?*

Three weeks earlier, Tibby and I had gotten home around the same time. She was my height and build, with brown hair and dark eyes. We stopped to talk in our garage, making small talk about the weather, the COVID-19 pandemic, and our building. Her poodle sat patiently at her feet. *I like this neighborhood,* she said almost to herself. *But living alone this year has been hard.*

I nodded sympathetically. *How old were you when you met Adam?* She wanted to know. My answer—twenty-nine—seemed disappointing. She was already older, she explained, and dating during the pandemic had been challenging.

When I went inside, I told Adam about our conversation. *She seemed kind of stressed,* I said as I opened a seltzer. Over the next few days, our conversation nagged at me. But I didn't see her again.

As I drove past the police cars parked outside my building a few weeks later, I half expected to find her walking her dog on the street. Inside, Adam had too much energy; he didn't know what to do with himself. A neighbor stood outside her door with a police officer, a glass of water in hand. *We're just waiting for the coroner now,* the officer explained. *Her brother went for a walk.* His voice sounded far away.

I made pasta so I would have something to do and sat at the kitchen table, the pesto pooling in my bowl. I always used too much. As I stared at the sauce, I remembered the dimpled senior who hung himself when I was a freshman in high school. They told us at an assembly on April Fool's Day, and for a millisecond I wondered if the act was a twisted prank. After school that day, I lay in my bed until dinner. My first month of college, another freshman jumped from the top floor of the library. I cried for weeks, unable to articulate why I was so affected by the death of a stranger. After each tragedy, I experienced big feelings. But I didn't know where to put them, so I numbed out with food, alcohol, and men until the intensity faded.

Tibby was different. Even though we had only spoken a handful of times, her pain had been palpable, written across her face the last time I had seen her. I related to her more than I wanted to admit. I related to all of them.

* * *

IT WAS THE first semester of my senior year of college, and I had been drinking before a football game I wasn't particularly invested in. It was an excuse to wear matching T-shirts, take pictures, and start drinking before noon. By 4:00 PM, we were drunk and starving. This was intentional: the less we ate, the sooner we would feel the effects of our drinks. But now, we needed food.

The football stadium was a thirty-minute walk from campus, and a friend had volunteered to be our designated driver. She loaded a few of us into her car like folding chairs and drove us back to the main part of campus. As I rested my head against the car window, I felt it: the sadness that sometimes threatened to swallow me up whole. *No, no, no,* I begged. Not now. Not here.

But it was too late. The closer we got to campus, the tighter my chest became. I tried to focus on my breathing, but I struggled to inhale, exhale, repeat. I was still heartbroken over my latest split from my on-again, off-again college sweetheart, and despite my best attempts, tailgating hadn't magically altered my feelings.

At my friend's apartment, I snuck a beer into the bathroom and dialed my ex-boyfriend's number. I had deleted it from my phone, but I knew it by heart. I could hear my friends in the living room making dinner plans and getting ready for all the parties happening that night. I stared at my reflection as I waited for him to answer. I heard he was already seeing someone new, and I needed to know if it was true. I took two long sips of beer before he picked up.

When I emerged from the bathroom, sadness had me by the throat. On the phone, when I asked about the rumor, he sounded delighted. His voice was cruel. *You really expect me to tell you if I'm seeing her or not?* He laughed. *She is hot though.*

I told my friends I was tired. *Lie to them,* sadness told me. I faked a yawn and left, walking home slowly like the main character in a sad music video.

In my room, I pulled up Facebook. I knew I would regret it in the morning, but I couldn't stop. At the time, Instagram still didn't exist. But social media was already becoming a new addiction; I reached for it when I wanted to escape. I used it as a tool to compare myself to girls from high school, people I had met during Freshman Orientation, friends of friends I had crossed paths with years earlier. Everyone seemed happier, better dressed, and cooler than me. Years later, a friend of mine would remind me my profile likely looked the same way to other people.

I started with my ex's profile and made my way to his tagged pictures. I knew them all by heart. I revisited the ones of the two of us: holding hands on campus, eating pizza in his hometown, kissing in front of the Rockefeller Christmas tree. From there, I clicked on the new girl he was apparently seeing. She was thinner and taller than me. Her Facebook status informed me that she was writing a thesis in Public Policy, which I determined made her brilliant and better than me in every way. As I scrolled through her pictures, I decided she was everything I wasn't. I alternated between her profile and my own, comparing the shapes of our eyes and thighs. I counted her photo albums; did I have too many or did she have too little? My tagged pictures showed a broad social circle, a different party every weekend. Hers revealed a close group of girlfriends drinking in their kitchen. I updated my profile picture to one of me on the beach then deleted it. She hadn't changed her profile picture in a year; I didn't want to seem like I was trying too hard. I refreshed her page, and a new tagged photo appeared. It had just been uploaded. There they were: my ex-boyfriend sitting in his living room, on the couch where he said he loved me for the first time. His arm was around her, and I started to cry.

The intensity of my feelings caught me off guard. I wasn't expecting it to hurt so much. I had broken up with him; we had started fighting constantly, and I wanted to enjoy my senior year of college. But now, seeing him with someone else, I wondered if I had made a mistake.

As I got up for the box of tissues, an object caught my

eye. There was a bottle of sleeping pills on my roommate's dresser. I had never paid much attention to them before, but suddenly they were all I could think about.

The sadness was acute, all consuming. I was drowning in it, and I imagined the pills dragging me to the surface, leaving me bobbing for a while. I would have done anything to erase the memory of that night; the way his voice had sounded as he laughed at me on the phone. I knew now that he had been with her when it happened. I poured a few pills into my palm and swallowed them before I could stop myself.

All at once, I was sober. I called my friend Hailey and told her what I had done. I tried to throw up, but nothing came. Then I sat down on my bed and waited.

I didn't know how much time had passed when I heard pounding on my door. It felt like hours, but it could have been minutes. Hailey was on the other side, flanked by two male friends. Both were students; one was an EMT, the other was a volunteer firefighter. Her face was pale, panicked. I tried to wave them off, but my slurred words were incoherent. They asked me questions and checked my dilated pupils. I felt very small as I began to cry. The EMT looked at me like I was the most pathetic person he had ever seen. Hailey took me by the arm and said I would sleep at her house. The next morning, she told me she had stayed up all night, monitoring my breathing as I slept in her bed.

I never told anyone what happened that night. When Hailey asked if I was okay, I told her I had just been really drunk. I was lying to both of us. I couldn't understand the sadness that had sprung up from nowhere and seized control of my thoughts and actions. Yes, I missed my ex-boyfriend. I was hurt he had moved on so quickly, and I was afraid of the future. But those emotions had felt so much bigger when I was drunk and alone in my dark room. They had hurt worse than anything I could imagine. At that moment, I hadn't thought of the outside world: my friends, my family, myself. All I wanted to do was numb the pain.

* * *

FOR THE BETTER part of my twenties, I used alcohol to edit my feelings in real time. When I quit drinking, I was sensitive and unsure. I apologized when the barista handed me the wrong coffee order. I went to work with the flu to avoid calling in sick. When I noticed someone had unfollowed me on social media, I wondered what I had done wrong. I sat on the train with headphones in my ears when nothing was playing. I felt like I was walking down a long beach, all eyes on me as I fidgeted with my bikini. And I archived and unarchived my Instagram posts daily.

In my recovery meetings, I heard a common refrain when someone new joined the group or celebrated a sober anniversary: *don't quit before the miracle happens.* I cringed every time. It sounded so trite.

And yet, as I counted days, and then months, without a drink, something miraculous really did start to happen. I began to feel relief. I slept soundly and remembered my dreams. When I laughed, I felt the vibration reach my cheeks.

I still had the urge to edit my feelings, but without alcohol, the desire was less consuming. I laced up my sneakers and went running in the park near my apartment. I noticed the way the sunlight slanted behind the trees, listened to the sound of Little League baseball practice, and watched goofy dogs chase tennis balls. I studied them all like a tableau until I remembered I was a part of their world too.

* * *

ON THE NIGHT the police found Tibby in her apartment, I took my dog for a long walk. I paid attention to the color of the sky, the way the breeze hit my arms and shimmied the leaves on the trees. When I got back to my building, I heard a voice coming from above my apartment. It took me a few seconds to register that it was Tibby's brother talking on the phone outside her apartment.

I hope you can do some of the things I couldn't. It sounded like he was reading to someone, his voice choking on tears. I put my key in the door. *Don't spend so much time in bed. Try to get more exercise. Find someone to love you. Learn to love yourself. And spend less time on social media.*

I opened and closed the door to my apartment quickly. My heart was racing; I felt like I had intruded on something sacred. When I told Adam what I had overheard, he shut his eyes, shaking his head. We spent the rest of the night with the television on, attempting to drown out the memory of Tibby's suicide note. Adam poured himself a large glass of wine, and then another.

Only later, alone in the bath, did I allow myself to re-play her words. I wiggled my toes and lay still, feeling the weight of what she had written. I had hardly known her; I had no idea what she had been going through. Still, as I imagined her spending days in bed, swiping on social media and feeling undeserving of love, my stomach lurched. I had skimmed the surface of those feelings, and I knew the darkness that lay underneath.

Getting sober wasn't a magic bullet, but it did give me space to feel the emotions I had been trying to erase since high school. I thought of my neighbor, the senior boy, and the freshman at the library. I thought of myself at twenty-one, scared and alone. I wished someone had told them all not to quit until their miracle happened. I reached for my phone instinctively, aching for a distraction. Then, I stopped. I was more than an avatar on a screen, and I didn't need to swipe, post, or archive my feelings. Instead, I could just be what I was: sad. It wouldn't last forever, and it wouldn't drag me under. I gripped onto the tub and let myself cry.

The root of an archiving binge is always the same: the desire to mask discomfort. Social media gives us an illusion of control over our lives, and nothing hits like archiving an old photo of you wearing an embarrassing outfit. But even when the feelings hit hard, they don't last forever. There is light on the other side of breakdowns, surprising moments of levity that feel impossible in the throes of pain.

When the desire to archive myself becomes overwhelming, I remind myself of all I am: a heartbeat, flesh and bone, a brain that remembers. Every day I wake up is an opportunity to start again. I know what it's like to want to disappear. But despite my best attempts at erasing myself, I'm still here. I didn't think I could get this lucky.

15

Wedding Planning and Champagne Problems

Before I stopped drinking, my past love interests ranged from emotionally unavailable to downright cruel. There was the Midwesterner who asked when I was going to pluck my eyebrows next, the fraternity president who had a girlfriend but texted me whenever he was drunk, and the venture capitalist who made me promise not to fall in love with him on our first date. It took me years of therapy to understand why I picked all the wrong men. I didn't believe I was worthy of love. When I stopped answering the late-night booty calls, I was ready to start healing. By then, I was already sober from alcohol, but it was clear toxic men were still holding me back from the freedom I so desperately wanted. So, I swore them off too. A year later, Adam came into my life.

Falling in love with him was like inching forward at

the start of a roller coaster. Up, up, up, my stomach waiting for the drop. Only it never came. Adam was steady, bright, and thoughtful. On our second date, he took the train to Carroll Gardens to put our name down at a tiny Italian restaurant that didn't take reservations, then turned back around, thirty minutes in the opposite direction, to pick me up. He read voraciously and loved nature. I had never been camping and recoiled at the sight of bugs; Adam identified flowers by name and took me blueberry picking in Maine. He set up a hummingbird feeder outside his bedroom window and gently pointed out stars in the night sky.

Unlike past relationships, I felt safe in Adam's presence. But the security was disorienting. All I had ever known was unpredictability in love, and sometimes I found myself wondering if it was all too good to be true. *I'm confused about why he's so nice to me,* I shared in my recovery meetings. I was used to chaos, and the calm made me nervous. I found myself distracted by intrusive thoughts when we were together. *Why is this so easy?*

My therapist suggested I find ways to anchor myself in the moment, so I started taking notes on my phone whenever Adam shared something he liked with me. *He loves maps, tea, bar games, passion fruit, calla lilies, animals (birds), trees, the cello.* For years, I had subsisted on scraps. Half memories of drunken dates and fragmented first kisses. Now that I was falling in love sober, the world was in Technicolor. I wanted to remember every bit of it.

Three months after we started dating, I picked a fight when he asked me to have dinner with his friends and their wives. He was a few years older than me, and most of his friends were married. *Just so you know, I'm not ready to get engaged,* I exclaimed frantically. He laughed and touched my cheek. *I know.*

As we fell deeper in love, my fears quieted. I was relieved when we disagreed or had difficult conversations, like when we discussed relocating to Los Angeles together. These exchanges were a sign this was not too good to be true; it was real. One morning, as he slept next to me, his body curled into mine, I realized that even in my most anxious moments, I had never questioned how he felt about me. He loved me the way I had never let myself be loved before.

When he proposed a year and a half after our first date, I looked down at him, waiting patiently on one knee, steady as ever. I smiled and touched his cheek. I was ready.

* * *

I HAVE NEVER been a planner in the traditional sense. I pack the night before vacations, forget to bring a jacket, and show up to important meetings with wet hair. When my cycling instructor tells the class how many hills and intervals he has planned for the next hour, I tune out. I don't want to know.

As our relationship continued to progress, Adam revealed himself to be my opposite in this area. He made reservations at new restaurants, booked plane tickets months in advance, and pre-ordered sneakers. When I tried to be romantic and plan our third date, I accidentally purchased movie tickets for the wrong night.

Looking too far into the future made me nervous; there were too many unknown variables. When I first quit drinking, I learned to take my sobriety one day at a time. *Just for today, I won't drink.* It was a reassuring refrain I began to apply to other areas of my life too. But *one day at a time* isn't as helpful when you use it as an excuse to put off important tasks like making doctor's appointments or going to the DMV. Adam's methodical planning was the perfect antidote to my anxious-avoidant style.

My hypothetical wedding was yet another event I avoided planning. Despite my extensive experience as a wedding guest, I had given very little thought to my own nuptials. Most of my friends had their wedding days mapped out before they even met their fiancés, but mine was a blank slate. This became apparent in the months after Adam proposed.

I had been to dozens of weddings since getting sober, and my relationship with them had evolved. In my first year of sobriety, I learned that being a wedding guest was no longer an excuse to party with an open bar or take pictures in a new dress. I paid attention to the vows, remembered how the food tasted, and listened to the speeches. I was a present guest, thrilled by the realization that attending someone else's wedding was not about me. It was about witnessing two people promising to love each other, for better or worse, with cake.

In years two and three, my rose-colored wedding goggles began to fog a little bit. As I grew more comfortable not drinking at weddings, my sobriety became less of a distraction. This created room for new experiences, both joyful and uncomfortable. I bickered with my date at a backyard wedding after they ran out of food. He turned to the bar for sustenance; I got hangry. At a country club wedding in New Jersey, I skipped dessert because I felt fat. The suburbs, I decided the next day, were terrible for my body image. When my friends and I got our makeup done for a fancy black-tie wedding in New York City, I made conversation with the artist. *It's been a stressful day,* he said as we finished. *Thanks for being kind.* When I was drinking or newly sober, I would have been too consumed with myself to connect. At a wedding in Australia, I found myself sobbing at the father-daughter dance, even though I had just met the bride. Sober weddings were a contained vehicle for my emotions. I felt a deeper range of joy, sadness, and fatigue after listening to vows and spending five hours in a pair of heels.

But the idea of my own wedding paralyzed me. Being the bride cast a spotlight on my insecurities, the smudges I tried to hide. I was still brokering a peace treaty with my body after years of disordered eating, and the thought of wearing a fitted white dress sent me into a panic. I could no longer comfort myself with the thought that no one would be paying attention to me: as a guest, this was true, but my wedding day was designed to be the opposite. I had no interest in planning a party, picking out china, or selecting floral arrangements. There were too many options, and they left me feeling both overwhelmed and disinterested. Adam and I went through various iterations of the day: a reception at a Brooklyn restaurant overlooking the city skyline, a small ceremony with my family in France, a minimalist marriage at City Hall followed by dinner with our closest friends. He jumped into planning mode, emailing vendors, securing quotes, and mocking up menus. I closed my eyes, trying on each version, but none of them felt right. I signed up for TikTok and made a video about why wedding planning was miserable. It got 25,000 views and a few defensive comments from brides. My resistance to it all made me feel insecure, like I was missing some crucial bride gene.

Then there was the drinking. Long before getting sober, I worried about the ramifications that not drinking might have on a future wedding. I couldn't imagine getting married without a champagne toast or enjoying my honeymoon without sipping on tropical cocktails. I knew getting sober was the only reason I had found a healthy relationship in the first place, but a tiny part of me was still worried my wedding wouldn't be as special without a celebratory drink. I used a tool I had been taught in early recovery and played the tape forward. Where would one glass of champagne lead?

(See: my wedding day with alcohol. I start the day with a mimosa or two as I get my hair and makeup done. By the ceremony, I'm buzzed. I'm proud of myself for not getting too drunk before cocktail hour, so I allow myself a glass of white wine, and then another. I haven't eaten. I stumble slightly through our first dance. During speeches, I toast with champagne before switching to tequila; it's my wedding after all. I ditch my heels and dance barefoot, before sloppily ordering a round of shots. My eyes go slack, and my forehead is sweaty; I haven't had any water. Toward the end of the reception, my brain turns off. My groom helps me back into the hotel room, wincing as I mumble nonsense. Maybe I make it to the bathroom, but I most likely throw up on my dress in our bridal suite. The next morning, I wake up in a panic. *Did I embarrass myself? How did the night end?* My first day as a wife, I am nauseous, agitated, and tending to a throbbing headache.)

I knew this scenario was entirely plausible because I had watched brides, even the ones who typically drank normally, overdo it at their weddings due to a combination of nerves, excitement, and an empty stomach. Their drunken merriment was well-intentioned, but I knew my own relationship with alcohol would not pair well with a white dress and a big party.

As I moved through my mixed feelings about having a wedding, time also continued to pass. One month went by, then three, and five. The coronavirus pandemic raged on, and we waited to see how vaccines would change the landscape of social gatherings. I would have married Adam on the spot, but it was important to him that we have a wedding with family and friends present. Still, I struggled to envision it all: the cheesy vows, the DJ, me, bronzed and impossibly toned, walking down the aisle in a big white wedding dress.

Luckily, I was marrying a man who continuously reminded me I could do and wear whatever I wanted on our wedding day. California was where we were building our new home, so we finally settled on a quiet mountain top an hour north of Los Angeles where people gathered to meditate. We made a small list of immediate family and close friends, a size that felt intimate but celebratory. I tried on dozens of wedding dresses and hated them all before finding a simple white dress that made me feel beautiful. In lieu of reading our own vows in front of our guests, we would write each other letters to read the morning of the wedding. And we found a jazz band that would not, under any circumstances, play "I Gotta Feeling" by the Black Eyed Peas. Adam, my thoughtful planner, mapped out the details: the flowers, the invitations, and the food and drinks, complete with a signature mocktail.

* * *

FIVE WEEKS BEFORE my wedding, I sat up in bed, panicked. I had my dress and shoes. Adam and I had signed our marriage license. I had even helped make some dinner reservations for the honeymoon. But what if I had forgotten to plan for marriage itself?

I sent a rambling email to every married relative and friend in my contacts list. *Will you send me your best marriage advice? The stuff you wish you knew in year one, how you navigate the ups and downs of life as a couple, and anything else that comes to mind?*

I was proud of myself for planning ahead, and I waited eagerly for my prize: a piece of life-changing advice that would signal I was prepared for marriage.

The responses trickled in, ranging from the romantic (*Just love each other!*) to more practical advice (*Hire a cleaner.*).

I pasted every response into a note on my phone and studied them like algebraic equations on the night before a test. My wise great-aunt, a woman who was raised in Morocco and never minced words, sent a matter-of-fact response: *Do not take at heart all the advice you'll be getting from left and right and all around . . . it's all Hollywood. A marriage is what you both make of it together.*

But I wanted more. I called my parents and they put me on speakerphone like they usually did when I was in crisis. I imagined them in the kitchen, exchanging a look as I asked them why they hadn't responded to my email. *You've been living together for two years,* my dad laughed. *You're pretty much already married.* I explained I was nervous I had forgotten to plan sufficiently for life as newlyweds. Even though I hadn't cared about picking the tablecloths or the chairs, I wanted to be a good partner. I wanted to plan for marriage.

Getting married is just the beginning, my dad finally said after a long pause. There would be bigger days, my parents explained, like when our babies were born or when we moved into our first house. There would be more time for planning, but there would also be plenty of space for stumbling along into the unknowns, together.

Still, I worried I was doing it all wrong. I turned to the externals, typing oddly specific phrases like *pre-wedding beauty timeline* and *best wedding nail polish* into Google. I was already too late; I should have started my bridal regimen twelve months earlier. I crowdsourced shoe recommendations and ignored everyone's suggestions. I showed friends pictures of my dress and overanalyzed their reactions. *You look happy in it, and that's all that matters,* a friend responded when I showed her my dress. *She hates it,* I told Adam definitively. But the problem wasn't the shoes or the vitamins or the friends. It wasn't even my lack of preparatory skills. It was my inability to surrender to the love being cast in my direction.

The year I turned seven, my parents threw me a birthday party at my favorite pizza parlor. I was excited for weeks, but the day of the party, my mood changed. I spent the afternoon in a frenzied state, convinced no one was having fun. I was incapable of relaxing and wound up in tears. In pictures from the day, my tiny friends are squished on either side of a decorated table, happily eating their slices. But my anxiety distorted my ability to see it all clearly. No matter how many times my mom told me, I didn't believe anyone wanted to be there celebrating me.

Just as I avoided planning birthday parties as an adult, I feared I would be disappointed by my wedding. I worried people wouldn't come, or worse, that they would wish they weren't there at all. The fear (of judgment, of neutrality, of boredom) was what kept me from planning, from letting myself get excited, from believing I was worth celebrating.

And then, it happened. My aunt, uncle, and three cousins in Paris announced they would be unable to travel to the States for the wedding. It wasn't their fault: in September 2021, America's borders remained closed to European travelers due to the COVID-19 pandemic, even those fully vaccinated. My family had hoped circumstances would change, but finally had to admit it looked unlikely.

I understood that, in a year of devastation, this was minor. Hundreds of thousands of people had died or lost loved ones since the start of the pandemic. I reminded myself of this fact and told everyone I was *fine*. But I was crushed. I threw myself a pity party and cried alone while walking my dog. Because of the small size of our wedding, my relatives in France were the only extended family invited to the wedding. My grandfather had passed away ten months earlier, and my grandmother couldn't travel due to her dementia. I told myself an old story: I was unworthy of love, wasn't worth celebrating, and wasn't enough.

After a week of isolating, I sent a text to my younger cousin, Pauline. I'm so sad you won't be able to come to the wedding, I wrote unhelpfully.

I'm so sad, she responded immediately. I can't even believe it. I always pictured your wedding and now it's happening, and we can't come.

I held my phone in silence, her broken heart emojis filling the screen. I had never thought about her envisioning my wedding or feeling disappointed about being unable to attend. I was grateful to remember that, yet again, my view of reality was inaccurate, skewed by my own self-centered fears.

Instead of texting my friends about shoes, I started sharing about my pre-wedding anxieties and sadness. The responses I received were a reminder that I was still loved. *It's devastating that your family can't come,* my therapist said. *But there are other people who can't wait to be there for you.*

I thought back to my parents at my seventh birthday party, my dad taping balloons to the table as my mom promised me everyone was happy to be there. I remembered my college friends making reservations for my birthday dinner, bringing cards and cake. I had people who wanted to be there for me, but my anxiety was obscuring my vision, blinding me to their love. All I could see were the ones who weren't there, and this distorted thinking was robbing me of joy.

My therapist and I decided I would give myself room to grieve those who were unable to attend my wedding, but also allow myself to enjoy the ones who were present. I could feel both, in moderation, without drinking or numbing myself. For the first time, I stuck to a plan.

* * *

IN ALL MY years of journaling, scheming, and dreaming, I never wrote about my dream wedding day. When I closed my eyes and tried to picture it all—the dress, the venue, the flowers—it was blank. I know now it's because I was still missing the biggest piece of all: him.

Don't get me wrong. My relationship didn't complete me. I did a lot of work on myself before I met Adam, and the work continues. But I am a better individual because of what I have learned about myself in our partnership. And in many ways, planning a wedding together was the ultimate group project. We practiced communicating, delegating tasks, compromising, and problem-solving. And when plans inevitably got altered, like our rehearsal dinner venue losing its license forty-eight hours before our wedding, we laughed. (After brief, respective breakdowns.)

In the end, on the Big Day, nothing and everything mattered. The dress, the flowers, the food, the music were all perfect and irrelevant compared to the fact that we were getting married. Like, for forever. If you think about it, it's sort of insane that two people can start out as perfect strangers and then decide to spend the rest of their lives together. As we stood under the chuppah, I thought about all the love stories that had come before ours: our great-grandparents, grandparents, and parents. Our rabbi read an excerpt from our Ketubah, the Jewish marriage contract we signed before the ceremony. Adam's eyes were bright with tears, and as I squeezed his hand, a hummingbird swooped down and hovered right above us, just for a second, before flying away. *We will remember why we fell in love,* the rabbi read, and I decide that, in all my remembering, I will also remember this.

* * *

THE YEAR I stopped drinking I told my therapist I didn't think I could do it forever. *How will I go to my wedding without having a glass of champagne?*

She looked confused for a moment. *Do you have a fiancé?* she asked, seriously. I told her no. *A boyfriend?* I shook my head.

Got it, she said, slowly. *Then maybe let's just wait and see how things go, shall we?*

See: my wedding day without alcohol, in which I sparkle without drinking any champagne.

I wake up early; my mom and I had a slumber party in my hotel room the night before. I go for a walk with my dad and drink an iced coffee. I read the card Adam gave me the night before in lieu of writing our own vows, and I feel deeply loved. I sit outside in the sun with a few of my sober girlfriends. I thank the universe for this day: I'm alive, I'm not hungover, and I'm sober. My body isn't bronzed or particularly toned, but it's healthy and mine.

My mom helps me into my dress; I wear a pair of her earrings and a blue lace garter that belonged to my grandmother. Adam's mom helps me with my shoes, and his sister snaps photos of us on her camera. I am so grateful not to be hungover or buzzed on mimosas at this moment.

We get married on a mountain. I walk down the aisle with both of my parents to the song I heard at the first wedding I attended when I was six. As "Only Wanna Be With You" by Hootie and the Blowfish starts to play, I see Adam standing under the chuppah wiping his eyes, and I start to cry. My mom beams to my right; my dad is steady on my left. I can't believe how happy I feel. For just a second, everything else stands still. The mountain range, our loved ones, my future husband. I didn't want a wedding, and I hated every second of planning it. But as I make my way down the aisle, my world in Technicolor, I am so glad I will remember all of it.

Our reception takes place on a grassy lawn surrounded by date palm trees. Adam and I gobble oysters and manage not to mess up our first dance. My dad gives a speech that makes me ugly cry. I sob as he tells the crowd how happy my grandparents would have been to be there with us, and as I look down at the delicate engraving in my wedding band—*Adam à Sarah,* the same phrase my grandparents wore through sixty years of marriage—I swear I feel them hug me. I watch our guests drinking wine, champagne, and Negronis, while I chug water. I'm honestly parched, anyway. As my friends pull me onto the dance floor, I am surprised, all over again, at how much fun I truly have without alcohol.

Being sober at my wedding feels like a superpower. The day doesn't go by in the blink of an eye; I am present for every second of it. I feel the joy rocket through my body, and I let myself take in the intensity. Afterward, I am exhausted for days, crashing from the aftereffects of the adrenaline. But I don't feel sadness when the wedding is over. I am ready for our marriage to begin.

* * *

TWO DAYS BEFORE getting married, I handed in the first draft of this manuscript. I split my time equally between writing and wedding prep, squeezing in workouts and meals and sleep. I ate mandarin oranges and squares of dark chocolate, refilled my water bottle, and typed.

It seemed fitting that the two biggest moments of my adult life had lined up in the same week. And each one was a perfect distraction from the other.

Aren't you freaking out? my friend Julia asked when she arrived in Los Angeles a week before the wedding. I wasn't sure if she was referring to the book or the wedding, so I shrugged.

I wrote with teeth whitening trays in my mouth, masks under my eyes, and my wedding planner on speakerphone. I squeezed the last drops of my single life onto the page— the bad dates, the blackouts, the messy nights, the hope— thanking each one of them for getting me to this place.

In many ways, this book was my bodyguard in the months leading up to my wedding. I had spent years internalizing the images of brides I saw on magazines and in social media, skeletal bodies, the aftermath of *shredding for the wedding*. Sure, I had years of recovery under my belt and a brain that knew better than to count calories and restrict my food intake. But the meatier defense against a diet was that I needed brain power for my life now. I couldn't think, write, or show up for anything if I was only operating on green juice. I needed substantial meals to be a person of substance.

I had spent a decade whittling my body down so I could see my collarbone in pictures. I weighed myself daily and wrote the figures down in my journal, treating my stomach like a science experiment. I photographed myself from every angle, studying the gap between my thighs and the width of my arms. I took pride in my ability to manipulate my outsides by skipping meals and spending an hour a day on the elliptical.

Being sober made my secret habits exhausting. I had given up alcohol so I could be free, but my obsession with being thin was keeping me in chains. When I asked myself how free I really wanted to be, the answer was clear. I had to let go of my grip on food and exercise to step fully into the rest of my life.

Still, my wedding photos surprised me. In the images, I looked full, like a woman. Initially, I recoiled at the site of my full chest and arms. *You should have tried harder,* my brain immediately screamed. *You should have skipped more meals.* But then, as I looked closer, the rest of the image came into focus. The look on Adam's face as he opened his arms for me. The smile that reached my eyes as I took his hand. The light that streamed through the trees as day turned to evening, marking the first hours we spent as husband and wife. These photos were our beginning, I realized, like the wedding albums on my grandparents' bookshelves. Our story wasn't about my body anymore: it was bigger than that. At my skinniest, I was my sickest. All I cared about was partying, and I was deeply lonely.

My life didn't look that way anymore. In sobriety, my body had expanded along with my capacity for joy. I had never seen anything more beautiful.

16

I Manifested This Book

I didn't know who I was, but I knew my way around New York City.

The city was a drug and I spent years getting high off it, ripping through subway tunnels in a trance. I didn't want to sit still, and New York was happy to help. There was always an event, a panel, a party, a lunch, a coffee date. I hopped in cabs and watched the city hurtle past me, the energy lulling me into a subdued state. I squeezed my body into bars and backlit rooftops where I drank the same watered-down vodka sodas and had the same conversations.

I've lived all over, I bragged to guys in bars who had just moved to the big city from Tennessee, Florida, Pennsylvania. I named my former neighborhoods like old friends, each one carrying the gravitas of history and acquired knowledge. *Midtown, Gramercy, Upper East Side, Williamsburg.*

I didn't mention that whenever I got off the subway at Union Square, I winced with the memory of my doorman putting me in an ambulance. I glossed over the uglier stories: tossing my cookies in trash cans in Central Park, Times Square, and the Lower East Side, too hungover to make it to a bathroom. I skipped the part about the shame I felt whenever I walked past an apartment complex I had mysteriously woken up in.

I was vaguely aware of the lies coming out of my mouth: I told people I was writing a book, deeply fulfilled by my job, thriving socially. Whenever I stopped long enough to ask myself if I was truly happy, Manhattan swept me away again.

In sobriety, the city provided a different kind of distraction. I still didn't want to sit still, and New York grabbed my hand and showed me what else was possible. There was always a meeting, a movie, and a diner open twenty-four hours a day. I saw New York with clear eyes and found myself falling in love with the city all over again. I was an emotional teenager enchanted by her crush: the way the early morning light hit the sidewalks, the sight of a yellow cab, and the endless cereal options at my corner bodega all filled me with glee.

Despite our hiccups, New York was a part of me. It was more than just where I lived; it was a main character in the story of who I had been and who I was becoming. Which is why I never expected to leave.

* * *

A YEAR AFTER I stopped drinking, I attended a manifestation workshop. It was one of those classic New York stories: a friend shared the event information and it just so happened to be taking place at a hotel a few blocks away from my apartment in Brooklyn. It was January, and one of my New Year's resolutions had been to remain open to new experiences. I wanted to prove to myself that the only thing I couldn't do was drink or do drugs; nothing else was off-limits.

Your goals you have for yourself can be set whenever, wherever you decide to make that conscious decision, the event description read. *Just ask Marika who, at last year's manifestation workshop, visualized owning a spacious, rustic apartment that she shared with a chiseled, blond man. Fast forward nine months and Marika owns a loft in South Street Seaport that she shares with her half-Scandinavian partner, Ryan. Dreams, or in this case, manifestations, do come true.*

A loft and chiseled man sounded promising. I purchased my ticket on the spot.

The workshop took place on January 19, 2019 (*We will be exactly 19 days into 2019,* the invitation stated ominously without clarifying why this was significant to the event). As I trekked through the snow that Saturday morning, I began to wonder what, exactly, I had signed myself up for. My friend had canceled at the last minute, and I had hardly ever meditated, much less manifested, before. I was happy with my life: I was sober, living in my own apartment in Brooklyn, and making six figures at my marketing job. My deepest desires, I thought, were to eventually be promoted to Chief Marketing Officer and spend my weekends strolling around the West Village with a lanky boyfriend. I wasn't sure I wanted kids or a husband, but I had my career and New York City.

As I walked into the hotel, a bright-eyed woman in her twenties smiled knowingly and directed me to the ballroom on the lower level. I cringed at what a cliché I was in my vintage jeans and tote bag; apparently, I had *manifests* written across my forehead.

The ballroom, a large space with a minimalist aesthetic and geometric architectural details, evoked a clean, cool sensation. Despite the snow outside, the air conditioning was on full blast; I wasn't sure if this was a design choice or an oversight. A single chair and microphone were positioned at the front of the room, facing out onto rows of folding chairs decorated with neatly arranged mini notebooks and pens. I sat in the middle of the room, surrounded by young women who looked just like me.

We are very lucky to have a world-renowned healer, clairvoyant intuitive, manifestation leader, and acupuncturist with us today, the event host emphasized in her introduction, and my twins and I all nodded in unison, feeling lucky. When our leader walked up to the microphone and smiled out at the crowd, we fell into a hushed, respectful silence. She had been in *Vogue,* after all.

The session began with a brief lesson on the three rules of manifestation, complete with a PowerPoint. Desire. Detach. Accept. First, she encouraged us to get extremely specific about our desires. *Visualize every detail about the dream job, the apartment, the marriage.* Next, once we allowed ourselves to identify our desires, we had to detach from them.

I call this the no fucks rule, she said. *You don't give your desire all your power or self-worth. You're fine without it. Desire is an extension of you, not bigger than you.* I took dutiful notes on the presentation as though I would be quizzed later. The last and most important rule of manifestation was accepting and receiving. She gave an example of a woman who had been manifesting a house. A few months later, her great-aunt passed away and left the house in her name. But it wasn't the home she had envisioned: it was run-down, far from the city, and would take ages to renovate. The woman was disappointed. *If we get too attached to a specific outcome, we miss subtle hints from the universe that our dreams are coming true.* When the woman accepted and received the house, her next step became clear: she sold the house and land and put that money toward her dream home.

Once the rules were laid out, we moved onto mantras. *Destruction always precedes creation,* the leader said, pausing to indicate this was something we should write down. We needed to examine our inner monologues and turn them into affirmations. I rolled my eyes, imagining talking to myself in the mirror every day. *It's okay if you think you're lying,* she said, piercing through my inner monologue. *But visualizing can materialize.* She described a study in which a basketball team was split in two: one half physically practiced, while the other group envisioned themselves getting the ball through the hoop. Visualizing and practicing had the same positive effect; all the players improved.

The same was true of the inverse. If I spent all my time beating myself up, I was materializing my unkind thoughts.

She had us make a list of our limiting beliefs in our little notebooks and then cross them out and turn them into positive statements. *I don't believe I can truly find happiness or connection. Something must be wrong with anyone who finds me interesting. My judgment when it comes to men is broken; I gravitate toward broken people who will hurt me. If I let someone in, they'll see that I'm unlovable.*

I crossed it all out. *I believe I will find happiness and connection,* I wrote. *Nothing is wrong with someone who finds me interesting. I trust my judgment when it comes to men because I know I can advocate for myself now that I am sober. I gravitate toward kind, genuine people who will love me.*

My limiting beliefs made me a little sad. Even at a year sober, I still didn't trust my judgment when it came to men. For so long I had been dating the wrong guys, blacking out with them, and spending time chasing after emotionally unavailable men who made me feel insignificant. Next, she encouraged us to shift our narrative to our professional limiting beliefs and do the same exercise.

I actually really want to write a book, but I can't do it. I'm not a good enough writer. No one wants to hear what I have to say and it's too big of an undertaking. I won't be able to ever finish it. Then I crossed it all out and wrote the opposite. We repeated this for a few more minutes.

Finally, the lights in the room lowered, signaling it was time to get Zen. Our leader explained that she was going to be taking us through a twenty-minute guided manifestation meditation designed to reveal our truest desires. In this meditation, we would be taken through a day five years in the future and get a glimpse of our dream lives; no vision was too outlandish. We were deserving, she reminded us gently. It was time to meet our future selves.

Envision yourself waking up in five years, she began, her voice husky and low. I lowered my head, letting my eyes shut. *Where are you? Take your time. What do you hear? What do you see?*

I expected to see myself waking up in a new apartment, the sounds of Manhattan seeping in through the walls, but my brain stalled. *Quiet your mind and let go of your expectations.* I cracked one eye open, wondering how she had read my mind. *Let yourself sink into this beautiful life that you have created for yourself.* I closed my eyes again. *Who are you waking up next to? How do you feel? Now let's start your day.*

* * *

I WAKE UP in a white room, morning light coming in through the open windows. The room is quiet, but I hear the slight rustling of a house around me. (*A house?*) I sit up in bed and look around. I'm in a bright bedroom with a wicker laundry basket and cozy white chair in the corner. I hear water running from the other room, and my husband walks out of the bathroom. I'm enveloped in a hug; I can't see his face, but I feel the warmth of his love. He is my best friend. A small dog jumps onto the bed and cuddles into me. I get out of bed and stand in front of the bathroom mirror. *How do you look? How do you feel?* When I see my face and body reflected at me, I realize I'm pregnant. I feel confident and at peace. *Continue walking through your morning.*

Downstairs, we move through an easy rhythm: coffee, breakfast, walking the dog. *What are you doing next? Let yourself soak in every detail of this day and your life.* I find my way into a room at the base of the staircase and open the door. Inside, I see a desk overlooking a window and a stack of books. *By Sarah Levy,* they say. I hold my first book in my hands and feel a pride I have never known. I am writing my second book.

I work for a while, and then I get in my car and drive through a quiet, sunny neighborhood to a recovery meeting. (And wait, am I living in California?) I am surrounded by familiar faces. I am a part of a community of sober women; I have the kinds of meaningful friendships I always looked for when I was drinking.

My family lives nearby, and my brother, who has been struggling with depression, is happy and healthy. My parents come over for dinner and we eat a big, delicious meal outside. Juice from my hamburger dribbles down my chin; I am not counting calories or restricting my food intake. At night, my husband and I read in bed and talk about our days. This weekend, we will go to the farmers' market and on a hike. We are close with our families. I write every day and have an editor who believes in me. I am present for my life, my relationship, my work, and my friends.

* * *

As THE MEDITATION ended, the leader invited us to come back into the room. She encouraged us to take a few minutes to write our meditations down, and I scribbled the above in my notebook, not wanting to forget a single detail.

When I finished writing, I was surprised to find tears in my eyes. A baby? A book? Me, the world's worst parker, driving confidently around *California*? It sounded almost trivial, not to mention worlds apart from the life I was building in New York. But I couldn't ignore the joy that had filled my belly as I imagined it all.

As the morning drew to a close, our manifestation queen told us to share our visions with our neighbors, introducing ourselves as our dream selves so we could speak them into existence. We all tittered nervously, but the energy in the room had shifted: I could tell we were all a little stunned by what we had seen. The girl next to me introduced herself as a small business owner who was living with her wife in Maine; another young woman shared that she had seen herself attending business school even though she was currently working in a creative field. I introduced myself as a writer. Everyone had a dream they thought was too big to come true, and yet they all sounded plausible to outside ears. *Now cheer for your future selves,* the leader shouted into the microphone. We blushed at the applause.

On my walk home, I replayed the last hour. It was no secret I had dreamed of being a writer since I was a little girl, but I always thought everyone shared the same fantasy, like being a pop star or an astronaut. I created a mental equation: if everyone else wanted to be an author, there was simply less of a chance I would make it as one. I busied myself with other, more realistic goals, and bit my lip every time I read about someone getting a new book deal. I wanted that, a little voice tried to pipe in, but I never let myself listen to it.

But as I thought about all the desires floating around that room, I realized there was no law preventing us from receiving them. If I believed the girl to my left could design jewelry, then why couldn't I write a book or start a family? There was no ceiling on love; no cap on collective success. What would happen, I wondered, if I believed in an abundance of opportunity instead of feeling like there was a scarcity of good opportunities available for me? How would my life change if I acted like there was limitless potential for new books to be written, rather than viewing bookstores like they were already at capacity, a symbol of my personal failure to launch? What if my life in New York, my obsession with my job title, my need to constantly be busy and in motion, was just me distracting myself from what I really wanted? What would it look like to take small steps toward that big, beautiful life I had envisioned walking through five years in the future?

I thought and thought, and then, I inadvertently followed the second rule of manifestation: detachment. I sort of forgot about it all. I went to yoga, had dinner with my parents, and edited a presentation for work. I promptly returned to my normal life, and it was enough.

I didn't know it then, but a seed had been planted. My subconscious had stirred, and something big was being set in motion.

* * *

EIGHT DAYS AFTER the manifestation workshop, I ran into a friend near Washington Square Park. We had met a few months earlier, and we began chatting casually. I had some time until my brunch, so I joined her group on their walk to Eva's Kitchen.

At Eva's, I ordered an orange juice and made my way to a small table with my friend. We were talking about our weekend plans when her phone went off. *Sorry,* she said, responding to a text message. She typed for a few seconds before looking up at me suddenly. *Are you seeing anyone?* she asked.

I shrugged. *Not really. Just random Bumble dates.*

I think I want to introduce you to this guy. She gestured at her phone as if a tiny man was living inside. They worked together, she explained, and rattled off a brief description. *Really nice, smart, cute. There's just one thing.* She paused. *He technically lives in LA. But he's back in New York all the time for work.*

Normally, I wouldn't have considered a setup with someone who lived on the other side of the country. What was the point? I wasn't looking for a pen pal. It didn't make logical sense. But something fluttered inside me, a tiny voice pushing me to say yes.

You can give him my number, I agreed before I could talk myself out of it. *A part-time boyfriend honestly might be nice.*

Who knows? I joked to my mom a couple of days later as I told her the story. *Maybe this is why I saw myself in California when I did that manifestation workshop.*

We both laughed.

* * *

THIS ISN'T A story about how meeting a guy was my happily ever after. It's an example of how sobriety cleared up the space in my brain and heart for my life to change. When I stopped making decisions based on fear, limiting beliefs, and judgment, everything started to shift.

After the manifestation workshop, I detached from my five-year desires, but I remembered the mantras. I didn't go full talking-to-myself-in-the-mirror, but I did start saying them in my head as I brushed my teeth or waited for the subway. *I believe I will find happiness. Nothing is wrong with someone who finds me interesting.*

When I met my prospective part-time boyfriend, it was clear he had full-time potential. Adam was kind, thoughtful, generous, and warm. On our second date, I mentioned I had been a huge Justin Timberlake fan since middle school. A couple of weeks later, he invited me to meet him in San Francisco; he had gotten us tickets to see Justin Timberlake in concert. Fear bubbled up. I had the urge to self-sabotage. *Why was he so nice? What was the catch?* A sober friend suggested I think of dating as information gathering and to observe my reactions with nonjudgmental curiosity. *You deserve someone nice,* she reminded me firmly. I remembered my mantra, and the joy I had felt after that meditation. Was this the part where I was supposed to accept and receive? I agreed to go to the concert.

When I was with Adam, I felt comfortable and excited at the same time. Other men I dated smiled politely when I told them about my love of writing. But this guy perked up. He asked to read my work, and I sent him the first freelance essay I had published a few months earlier about how dating without alcohol made me feel like an awkward teenager. I briefly worried my vulnerability in the piece would scare him off, but he commended the honesty and said the writing was smart and funny.

He encouraged me to pitch more freelance stories, and I let myself imagine what they might look like. We spent lazy weekend afternoons reading together in the park, and he brought me coffee in bed while I wrote. When I shared my biggest dream of all with him—writing a real book—he smiled like it was the best idea he had ever heard. His complete and utter faith in me brought back the ambition I had shelved in high school, right around my first drink. Being a writer was hard, I had decided back then; getting drunk was easier. Now that I was sober, I felt like I was getting a second chance.

As I began to write my way into a new plotline, I started to feel less tethered to New York. It still held me in the palm of its hand, but its grip became looser. I had hardly left the city when I was drinking; now I was increasingly aware of how much of the world I had left to see. I journaled about the places I wanted to go: Greece, Australia, Bali, Croatia, Spain. I wanted to walk on the beach without a hangover and get on a plane without needing sleeping pills. Every time I identified and articulated a new desire, I detached from it. It felt good to let myself dream, but none of it was urgent.

Two months later, Adam called with a question: did I want to go to Paris and Greece that summer? We could spend a few days visiting my grandparents in France, and then explore the Greek islands. Again, fear clocked me over the head. *Was a European trip too soon?* I asked my friends. *Why did this guy like me so much? When was the other shoe going to drop?* I flashed on my dream destination list, tucked away in my journal unbeknownst to him, and let myself say yes. That fall, he invited me to attend his friend's wedding with him; it just so happened to be in Australia. Every small step I took out of my comfort zone stemmed from the trust I was building in myself—and my manifestations.

A year after we met, I took Adam to the third annual New Year, New You manifestation workshop: same leader, same Brooklyn hotel ballroom. *I manifested you into existence,* I teased him often, *you weren't even real before that day!* At the event, we decided to sit separately so we wouldn't be distracted. I wondered if he would think the whole premise was cheesy or if he would give it a real chance. As the meditation started, I stole a few glances at the back of his head to see if he was doing it right.

Afterward, over donuts at a nearby coffee shop, I took a deep breath and asked him what he had seen in his meditation. His face was flushed from the cold, and the air smelled like sugar and espresso. I breathed it all in as we connected both parts of the story we were already writing together.

* * *

MANIFESTATION ISN'T A WOO-WOO trend. It's a lesson in reallocating time and energy. My first manifestation workshop helped me identify a goal, and now I had a choice: I could start walking toward it, or I could stay in place. The shifts were gradual and hinged on small daily actions, much like my journey to sobriety. I started journaling again. I jotted down story ideas on the subway. I spent time with friends who reminded me I was deserving of love and kindness. I said yes to another date with a nice guy. I sent out freelance pitches. I started outlining a book. One step at a time, I found myself moving toward a new life.

But manifestation doesn't preclude you from fear. Even though I had seen myself thriving in California in the future, my present self was terrified to leave New York. When Adam and I first discussed moving to Los Angeles, I told him I wasn't sure. I didn't know if I was ready to say goodbye to my bodega, the L train, or University Place. We took a trip to LA, a city I had only briefly visited once before, and I tried to envision my life there. I took long sunny walks and tried to find public transportation and called my friend Britni asking if I was making a mistake. I was scared as hell. But I also felt something familiar fluttering, a tug toward the unknown. *Relationships are about compromise,* Britni said, reminding me of all the trips Adam had taken to New York when we were first dating. *Maybe it's your turn to show him you're in this too. And you can always move back.* I told him I'd give it a try.

When we moved to LA at the start of summer, I was confused by the quiet. I didn't know where anything was, what the highways were called, or how to parallel park. I studied maps and had a panic attack the first time I drove at night. I was wide awake, more present than I had been in my entire life and blinded by all the sunshine. I craved the comfort of New York in all its noisy, messy glory. *I knew who I was in New York. I knew every subway line by heart and had a favorite restaurant in every neighborhood,* I whined to my therapist. *I hate how lost I feel here.*

When we move to a new city, sometimes we become obsessed with feeling completely settled, she said. *But when we rush ahead, we miss out on the joy of novelty.*

In my wildest dreams, I always envisioned myself as established, secure, and content. But if manifestation and sobriety had taught me anything, it was that finding contentment took time and patience. So, I started taking small steps. I found a hiking trail with an easy parking situation. I reached out to friends of friends for coffee. Adam came home with a stack of books about California, and I started to learn about my new city.

The summer after I moved to California, I visited New York again. The city felt different; tougher somehow. After dinner with friends, I moved through the West Village, carried by the current of bodies and energy. We stood at the intersection of a crowded Bleecker Street littered with twenty-somethings just starting their nights and stories. Their cheeks were flushed: from cocktails, humidity, and possibility. I remembered all the nights I moved with them, letting the city thrum in my ears, my cramped apartment filled with plastic storage bins and an overcrowded bookshelf. I was both jealous of them and happy. This chapter of my life was over, but New York was still there, a symphony of car horns and traffic cheering me on, reminding me of who I had been and where I was going.

I thought about my life in Los Angeles: my white bedroom,

the sunlight, the quiet corner where I wrote every morning. The contrast was stark between my secure existence in New York and the unfamiliar one I was building in California. I wasn't five years into the future yet, but I was making my way toward everything I had envisioned, one small step at a time. Manifestation had taught me how to do that.

Back on Bleecker, my friend Lara sighed. *Think of all the lives lived on this one corner,* she said, almost to herself, as we crossed the street. I didn't tell her I already was.

* * *

WITHOUT SOBRIETY, *MANIFESTATION* would have been an empty buzzword for me. Getting sober made space for me to focus on what I truly wanted from my life, and manifestation gave me the tools to articulate it all.

There is a meditation I return to often. The title (*Your future self now: visualize to materialize*) is almost painfully corny, but it has an immediate, grounding effect. Even though I no longer drink alcohol, I still wake up every day feeling a little bit drunk. The bully in my head wakes up a few minutes before me, and she's ready to tell me everything I'm already doing wrong by the time I join her. *You're late, you're lazy, no one likes you.* Coffee is obviously nonnegotiable, but I also need to journal, go for a walk, and meditate to shake the mean girl out.

My manifestation meditations guide me back in the direction I'm supposed to be headed. I need a steady, measured voice to ask me the questions I answered yesterday about where I see myself going. *Imagine your manifestation actualizing.* As I move myself into the future, my subconscious mind falls in line. Even my inner mean girl is a rule follower, and we do what the guiding voice tells us to. We envision our big future dreams, and express gratitude for the present. And when I open my eyes for the second time that day, I finally feel grounded.

Today, I am the future self I envisioned years ago. My life is hardly perfect, but I am present for it because of the clarity sobriety has given me. I have felt pure joy, formed authentic connections, moved through devastating loss, and experienced true love. If nothing else ever changed for me, this would be enough. Because once upon a time, all I ever wanted was to stop blacking out. To wake up with memories from the night before and possess the confidence that I could form relationships without alcohol. Somehow, I got so much more than I ever bargained for. And still, I can't help but dare to wonder what's yet to come.

Conclusion

What Comes Next

My wish for this book is that it reaches someone who needs it. Maybe you don't think you can have a *real* drinking problem because you're twenty-three and all your friends party too. I was you. Maybe you roll over at 4:00 AM and pick up your phone, searching #sober on social media because you're trying to find someone, anyone, to talk to. I was you. Maybe you're lonely, sick of binge drinking, and tired of spending your weekends hungover. Maybe you want more meaningful relationships with your friends and family, or you're ready to give up gossiping, lying, and keeping secrets. Maybe you want more from your life, but you don't know whether you can do it. I was you. I'm still you.

No one can tell you whether you "qualify" for sobriety.

Only you can decide that. But if you do decide to give it a try, know that you're not alone.

Some people celebrate sober anniversaries; others call them birthdays. *I'm five!* people exclaim when they achieve five years of continuous sobriety. The birthday metaphor checks out. In my first few years of sobriety, I rediscovered the kind of emotions I had only felt as a young child. I stood silently in nature, gobsmacked by the beauty of oceans, mountains, and starry skies. I laughed until my stomach hurt, flooded with the contagious giggles that are impossible to shush. I sobbed myself to sleep. I felt joy so explosive that I found myself skipping down sidewalks with ABBA blasting in my headphones, my dog trotting happily beside me (okay, in retrospect this last one was probably mildly dangerous).

At five years sober, I still do things I know might make me feel terrible afterward, like eating Sour Patch Kids before dinner or drinking three coffees a day. I watch more TV than I should and spend way too much time on my phone. I have a stack of unread books on my nightstand and leave mail unopened on my countertop for days. I put off making dentist appointments and hate folding laundry. But I don't drink. And on days when that's the only thing that goes right, it's enough.

What now? I sometimes find myself wondering. The answer, in sobriety, is simple: anything.

ACKNOWLEDGMENTS

I want to thank my parents first and foremost. Thank you for reading everything I've ever written, for being my editors, cheerleaders, and role models, and for teaching me to have a strong work ethic and be kind. Thank you for investing in my education and future, even when it meant making sacrifices, and for encouraging me to pursue this dream. I am the luckiest to have you both.

Thank you to my literary agent, Kristyn Keene Benton, for believing in the idea for this book and championing it so fiercely. I am so grateful for you. Thank you to my editor, Sallie Lotz, for being so dedicated to this project, understanding what I want to say before I've written it, and becoming a dear friend. This book is a million times better because of you and your brain. I also want to thank everyone at St. Martin's Press for supporting this book at every stage: Sarah Cantin, Laura Clark, Jennifer Enderlin, Jessica Zimmerman, Allison Ziegler, Katie Bassel, and Olga Grlic.

Thank you to the rest of my team at ICM/CAA, especially Alicia Gordon for teaching me so much about this crazy world they call show business.

Thank you to Joanna Goddard of *Cup of Jo* for publishing the essay that set this book in motion.

I want to thank the incredible teachers and mentors I've had over the years: Kevin Wittmaack, Mark Stern, Freddie Glucksman, Susan Rothbard, Darcey Steinke, and Jenny Han. Thank you also to Amie Karp for teaching me how to heal.

To my friends: thank you for being a safe place to land. For all the leisurely dinners, weekend trips, long talks, coffee dates, workout classes, FaceTime sessions, car rides, outfit recommendations, laughter, and advice. I love you all.

To all the women in and out of recovery rooms who loved me until I learned to love myself: I could not have done any of this without you. You know who you are. I also want to thank everyone who sent me emails and messages about your own sober journeys. I see you; you're not alone.

I feel so fortunate to have married into such a loving and supportive family. Thank you to Cindi, Richard, Jamie, and Janet for making me feel so welcome from day one.

Thank you to my brother, Eric, for always having my back and reading every draft of this book. Being your sister is the best gift Mom and Dad ever gave me.

Thank you to my grandparents, Liliane and Ruben Levy, for instilling a love of family, reading, and storytelling

in me. I know this book would have lived front and center on your bookshelf. *Je vous aime beaucoup, beaucoup.*

And a very special thank-you to my husband, Adam: You're the best thing I've ever manifested. Thank you for your unwavering love and support, all the home-cooked meals, and being the best dog dad imaginable. I'm so proud of this life we're co-writing together.